The Sustainability Effect

The Sustainability Effect

Rethinking Corporate Reputation in the 21st Century

Arlo. Kristjan O. Brady

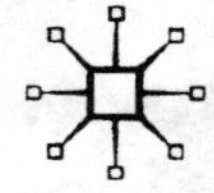

First published in 2005 by
PALGRAVE MACMILLAN
Houndmills, Basingstoke, Hampshire RG21 6XS and
175 Fifth Avenue, New York, N.Y. 10010
Companies and representatives throughout the world.

PALGRAVE MACMILLAN is the global academic imprint of the Palgrave Macmillan division of St. Martin's Press, LLC and of Palgrave Macmillan Ltd. Macmillan® is a registered trademark in the United States, United Kingdom and other countries. Palgrave is a registered trademark in the European Union and other countries.

ISBN-13: 978–1–4039–9171–3 hardback
ISBN-10: 1–4039–9171–5 hardback

This book is printed on paper suitable for recycling and made from fully managed and sustained forest sources.

A catalogue record for this book is available from the British Library.

Library of Congress Cataloging-in-Publication Data

Brady, Arlo Kristjan O., 1977–
The sustainability effect : rethinking corporate reputation in the 21st century / by Arlo Kristjan O. Brady.
p. cm.
Includes bibliographical references and index.
ISBN 1–4039–9171–5 (cloth)
1. Corporate image. 2. Sustainable development. 3. Social responsibility of business. I. Title.

HD59.2.B73 2005
658.4'083—dc22 2005046323

10 9 8 7 6 5 4 3 2 1
14 13 12 11 10 09 08 07 06 05

Printed and bound in Great Britain by
Antony Rowe Ltd, Chippenham and Eastbourne

To my parents

Contents

List of Tables

List of Figures

List of Charts

List of Abbreviations

AIDS	Acquired Immunodeficiency Syndrome
BBC	British Broadcasting Corporation
BP	British Petroleum – or – Beyond Petroleum!
BSC	British Safety Council
BSI	British Standards Institute
Co_2	Carbon dioxide
CALpers	California Public Employees Retirement System
CARB	California Air Resources Board
CBA	Cost–Benefit Analysis
CBI	Confederation of British Industry
CC	Corporate Citizenship
CBD	Convention on Biological Diversity
CEO	Chief Executive Officer
CES	Corporate Environmental Strategy
CIA	Central Intelligence Agency
CR	Corporate Responsibility
CSR	Corporate Social Responsibility
DDT	Dichlorodiphenyltrichloroethane
DEFRA	Department for the Environment, Food and Rural Affairs
DTI	Department for Trade and Industry
EC	Environmental Credibility
EM	Emotional Connections
EMAS	The Eco-Management and Audit Scheme
ESG	Environmental, Social and corporate Governance
EU	European Union
FC	Financial Credibility
FMA	First Mover Advantage
GBN	Global Business Network
GF500	Global Fortune 500
GM	General Motors Corporation
GNP	gross national product
GRI	Global Reporting Initiative
GSK	GlaxoSmithKline
HBR	Harvard Business Review
HFC	Hydrofluorocarbons

HIV	Human Immunodeficiency Virus
IISD	International Institute for Sustainable Development
ISO	International Standards Organisation
KS	Knowledge and Skills
KPI	Key Performance Indicators
LV	Leadership, Vision and Desire
MNC	Multinational Corporation
NASA	National Aeronautics and Space Administration
NGO	Non-governmental Organisation
NYU	New York University
PA	Personal Assistant
PR	Public Relations
PwC	PricewaterhouseCoopers
RBV	Resource Based View
RQ	Reputational Quotient
SC	Social Credibility
SIGMA	Sustainability: Integrated Guidelines for Management
SMA	Second Mover Advantage
SME	Small to Medium size Enterprise
SRI	Socially Responsible Investment
SUV	Sports Utility Vehicle
TBL	Triple Bottom Line
TDM	Dillman's Total Design Method
TRI	Toxic Release Inventory
TRIPs	Trade Related Intellectual Property Rights
UK	United Kingdom
UN	United Nations
UNCSD	United Nations Commission on Sustainable Development
UNEP	United Nations Environment Programme
UNFCCC	United Nations Framework Convention on Climate Change
UNICEF	United Nations Children's Fund
US$	United States Dollar
US, USA	United States
WBCSD	World Business Council for Sustainable Development
WCED	World Commission on Environment and Development
WEF	World Economic Forum
WRI	World Resources Institute
WTO	World Trade Organisation
ZEF	Zero Emissions Fuel Mandate

Acknowledgements

This book would not have made it out of the confines of my head without the inspiration, insight, help and downright patience of a small group of people. Most of all I would like to thank my family and in particular my sage and sounding-board Dr Alessandra Buonfino. I would also like to extend my heartfelt gratitude to Dr Chris Hope and Prof. Peter Guthrie from Cambridge University and Prof. Rod Aspinwall from the British Sustainable Development Commission.

Special thanks are also due to Prof. Dame Sandra Dawson for giving me the opportunity to interact with the superb group of brains that she has assembled and calls the 'Judge Institute', to Sir Mark-Moody Stuart at Anglo-American for having helped me with my research and provided comments on parts of this book; to Jason, Dan, Ian, Dave, Alex and Evelin at Sd3 for giving me the opportunity to work with them and their clients for the last five years and finally to Dr Paul Ashley and my team at Mott MacDonald who have given me a head start on what I freely admit is a steep learning curve.

Extracts of this book have previously been published and presented at various forums including at the European Academy of Business in Society, the Conference Board, Euro-Sustainability, the Reputation Institute, *CES the International Journal of Corporate Sustainability, Ethical Corporation Magazine, Corporate Responsibility Management*, the *Journal of Brand Management* and *Sustain Magazine*. I would like to thank the editors and reviewers from the above publications and organisations.

Various individuals have, perhaps unwittingly, inspired me and influenced my thinking at stages over the last three years. I would like to thank Dr David Deephouse (University of Alberta) and Professor John F. Mahon (University of Maine). Dr Kristin Zimmerman (General Motors), Dr Kai Hockerts (INSEAD), Professor John Stopford (LBS), Dr Chris J. Moon (CSR Global), David Vidal (Conference Board), Professor Malcolm McIntosh (University of Bath), Joss Tantram (Terra Consult), Vesa Kangaslahti (Cambridge), Jim Collins, Dr Simon Zadek (AccountAbility) and Andrew Wilson (Ashridge).

I should say that while many individuals have helped me to reach this point, one individual alone is responsible for the content and that is, of course, me.

Preface

Corporate sustainability, responsibility and citizenship are rapidly entering the global business lexicon. Yet despite this there has been little detailed research designed to examine corporate reasoning, response and behaviour. This book is grounded in research designed to address specific aspects of these questions. As such, I hope that its readership will be composed of both corporate decision makers, and also others whose interests lie in research. In particular, I hope that a portion of the readership will be composed of 'sceptics'. In my opinion, to a large extent, much of the current debate about these so called 'soft' business issues is taking place behind closed doors. In many ways it is often portrayed as a quasi-religious confrontation between the 'believers' and the 'disbelievers'. As with all things there is certainly a middle way, and I think that this is where real progress can be made.

This book will show the reader with a business background how to mitigate sustainability related risks and it will highlight some of the opportunities that can be capitalised upon in order to create competitive advantage. In contrast to other works in this area I have not suggested that reputation is a concept to be exploited, rather I have taken a practical approach making it clear that reputation can only be mobilised to one's advantage if one has genuine underlying holistic performance.

For the researcher or academic this book presents the detailed results of a research programme that I conducted over the last few years. On top of presenting the results and conclusions I have also taken care to emphasise those aspects which I believe contributed to its success, and areas where I thought my research technique could be improved.

As a last thought I would like to point out that through the course of my research and consultancy it has become apparent to me that while corporate responsibility and citizenship are controversial topics (hampering their universal uptake) – individual responsibility and citizenship are not. If you are socially and environmentally minded get out there and influence consumption and spending patterns. At the end of the day it is at the grassroots level where the real change truly lies. Don't just blame someone else!

1
Introduction

This book is the result of several years' research that was conducted at Judge Business School, University of Cambridge, between 2000 and 2004. It reflects the findings of a Global Fortune 500 CEO survey, but it also reflects the findings of a literature and practice survey and many of my experiences gained while consulting on sustainability issues for a number of prominent multinational corporations (MNCs).

The book offers a novel perspective on the corporate sustainability debate but, unfortunately, and unlike many others, it cannot claim to offer a clear solution. Over the last few years I have increasingly come to the realisation that this area is a minefield of complexity and dilemmas. It is not black and white, or to use the frequently espoused discourse of the corporate responsibility movement; a galactic battle between 'Good Corporation' and 'Bad Corporation'. I argue that this 'Phantom Menace' debate does little other than to damage the serious business case for sustainability. In reality it is a battle of multiple, and often competing dilemmas that companies and their stakeholders must join forces to resolve. The resolutions will not meet with everyone's approval – but will ultimately help contribute towards the societal goal of sustainable development. Many of the observations, proposals and conclusions that I make in the latter half of this book are based on the results of the survey that I conducted in 2002. The survey employed scenario planning techniques as tools to gain an original and slightly unconventional insight into the perceived future impact of sustainable development on the reputation of large MNCs.

The objective of asking this question was not necessarily to determine the *exact* impact – as due to the number of variables, this would be virtually impossible – but to establish the perception of global corporate leaders.

When interviewed on the television, radio, or when profiled by a newspaper, global corporate leadership can always be relied upon to say the correct thing. Through the usage of a strict privacy/confidentiality statement, the research sought to lift the veil of political correctness – exposing what experienced corporate leaders *really* deem to be the future importance of environmental and social credibility. By determining their perceptions we can expect to gain an insight into the potential direction of corporate sustainability strategy over the coming years.

We already know that a large portion of a company's value is made up of intangibles – various studies suggest that this can be up to 70 per cent of total value (for a review of these studies see Grey, 2001). For business, it is important to attempt to predict how, and to what extent, environmental and social credibility will/could impact this: Through dialogue with global leaders, this research reveals the extent to which corporate reputation is perceived to represent the *fabled return on responsibility* in the near future. It is of critical importance for me to concede that the field of research is young, intensely dynamic and due to its interdisciplinary nature inherently controversial. I was aware of this from the outset.

Bearing this in mind, I believe that the reader should be aware of my background; as a geologist turned environmental technologist turned business advisor, my perspective is not rooted in any one discipline. As a consequence, there are probably aspects of Chapters 2 and 3 that are not as detailed as a reader from a single discipline may expect. This is not a function of a lack of focus nor does it deter from its contribution; it is a deliberate function of the desire to maintain an objective perspective.[1] This is most evident in sections of this book. A traditional literature review would reveal such a level of discrepancy that it would be unintelligible and its practical use would not go beyond a mere encyclopaedic, backward looking, listing. Instead the section seeks to draw together current thinking – focusing on similarities as opposed to differences. New developments, controversies and breakthroughs within what are sometimes competing disciplines are critically discussed and bound together. This process of binding has brought to light several new notions and concepts which are worthy of interest and credence in their own right – not withstanding later, more traditional empirical work.

By contributing an incremental step in our understanding of the interface between business, society and the environment and reputation management it is hoped that the agenda can move forward with greater transparency and perhaps have a greater impact on the mammoth challenge that is Sustainable Development.

1.1 Layout

This book has been laid out in such a way that it is possible to read it straight through from start to finish, or to dip in and out using the contents or index as a point of reference. Without wishing to take away from the importance or interest of the other chapters I would recommend that the busy executive, with little time to spare, concentrates on Chapters 2, 3, 5, and 6.

This book is subdivided into 6 chapters. Leaving aside the introduction, the Chapter 2 addresses the phenomenon that I have termed 'Corporate Conscientiousness'. This phrase has not been used with the intention of adding to the already burgeoning market for acronyms in this field, rather it is an umbrella term that helps to describe a whole set of processes that are occurring at the interface between business, society and the environment. Following this literature, thought and practice review, Chapter 3 uses the same process to examine current thinking and corporate practice with respect to the construction of corporate reputations and imagery. Chapters 4 and 5 go through the methodology, content and results of a unique *Global Fortune 500* CEO survey. The survey used scenario planning techniques as a tool to gain an original and slightly unconventional insight into the perceived future impact of sustainable development on the reputation of large MNCs.

Chapter 6 presents the conclusions of this book in two separate ways. First, I have formulated 10 key propositions. These focus heavily on leadership for sustainability, long-term thinking, communication and partnerships. Second, I have highlighted a number of transitions inherent in the dynamic relationship between today's large MNCs and society (argued on the basis of a combination of the results of my survey with the literature and practice reviews in Chapters 2 and 3). I argue that the successful management of these seven transitions is essential to the extraction of reputational value from sustainability. This conclusion distils each of these directional changes and in doing so, presents a unique, challenging and revealing agenda for business and academia to further investigate/attempt to resolve.

2 The Rise of Corporate Conscientiousness

2.1 Introduction

> Never doubt that a small group of thoughtful, committed citizens can change the world; indeed, it's the only thing that ever does.
>
> Margaret Mead (1901–78) US anthropologist

This chapter charts the rise and implications of corporate interest/engagement in responsibility. After a brief introduction the theoretical framework underlying Sustainable Development is introduced in its historical perspective. This is followed by a discussion about what Sustainable Development really means to business, paying particular attention to the most popular models of implementation. Subsequently, three primary drivers of responsible behaviour are introduced and examined. Section 2.4 looks at the ways in which companies are demonstrating their responsibility performance and reviews some of the emerging guidelines.

2.2 People, the planet and profits

> Profits and principles, does there have to be a choice?
>
> (Shell International, 1998)

> People, planet & profits: an act of commitment.
>
> (Shell International, 1999)

A complex question, followed up by a statement of intent. These are the titles of Shell annual sustainability reports – published consecutively for the past seven years.

But, why are oil companies and many of their peers actively talking about people and the planet? What has happened in the last few years to ignite this apparent conscientiousness?

The answer is worryingly simple; the foundations upon which our economy is built are no longer looking completely adequate and people are starting to express their discontent.[2] As Laszlo points out; 'in the opening years of the twenty-first century we are launched on a process of profound and irreversible transformation' (Laszlo, 2001). Following the dramatic collapse of Communism in the late 1980s Neo-Liberalism and its stablemate Capitalism have achieved a position of unopposed ideological supremacy. Globalisation as a phenomenon has traversed the globe bringing benefits to some but desolation and deprivation to many more (Klein, 2000; Palast, 2002; Stiglitz, 2003).

Desertification, deforestation, climate change (or chaos), local air pollution, declining biodiversity and ozone degradation are just some of the key, pressing, issues that scientists have identified as being detrimental to the environment within which we live. The delicate and interwoven biological and chemical systems that are the basis of life on earth are being put in jeopardy. Using ecological footprinting methodology,[3] research done by the US National Academy of Sciences has shown that in 1999 the human economy (primarily based in the developed world) was absorbing 120 per cent of the Earth's productive capacity. This is compared with 70 per cent in 1961 (Wackernagel *et al.*, 2002). Worldwide, they estimated that the biologically productive space available per person is 5.4 acres; the average British citizen demands 13.34 and the average American citizen demands 23.97 (ibid). Each year we continue to demand more. This unsustainable state of affairs suggests that 'business-as-usual is ... on the track to environmental disaster' (Ayres, 2003).

However, it is not just our environment that is in trouble. The figures show considerable variation but according to a fact sheet published for the 2002 World Summit on Sustainable Development, 'there are 1.2 billion people living on less than one dollar a day, and about half the world's population lives on less than two dollars a day. With few choices or opportunities, they are condemned to lives that are prone to hunger, disease, illiteracy, joblessness and hopelessness. Too often, they lack access to food, safe drinking water, sanitation, education, health care and modern energy services' (World Summit on Sustainable Development, 2002).

These trends are not sudden, or unpredicted: over the past 40 years numerous high-profile studies have eloquently reminded us of these issues (for an early example see, Meadows, 1972). Why are we re-developing our concern now, all of a sudden, after the bull markets and dramatic

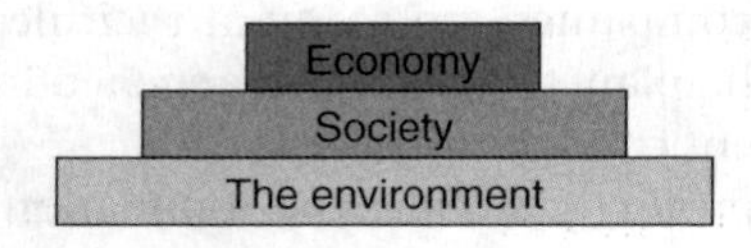

Figure 2.1 The pyramidal interrelationship between economy, society and the environment.

rise in consumerism of the 1980s and 1990s?[4] What has changed? I suggest that by virtue of the 'global goldfish bowl[5] the prosperous developed world is now able to observe the effects of this degradation first hand: the effects of war,[6] environmental destruction, famine and disease are now discernible in great detail and in real-time. Equally, the tragic events in the United States on 11 September 2001 were considered by many as a watershed moment; they, perhaps unwittingly, made it clear to the beneficiaries of globalisation that the world is implicitly interconnected and inequity and global injustice cannot simply be ignored (Muller-Kraenner, 2002; Soros, 2002). The issues have come to our doorstep and we are finding ourselves asking first who is responsible, and second what can be done to ameliorate or reverse the consequences.

Many governments, companies and individuals alike have been forced to take a step back, in doing this they seem to be coming to the fundamental realisation that society only thrives because of the environment within which it is seated. In turn, the economy, powered by the environment (in the form of resource consumption) thrives on a healthy society (see Figure 2.1).

This chapter traverses several practical and academic fields (some arguably more developed than others) in order to explore in detail the dynamic interrelationship between economy, society and the environment, with particular emphasis being paid to the evolving role of business. It asks if we are really witnessing a rise of 'corporate conscientiousness', and if so, what is driving it, and what form does it take.

2.3 Sustainable Development

Sustainable Development; as with many new ideas, is without a doubt far easier to write about than it is to actually 'do' or apply. This is because, as a concept, it represents a journey, not a destination. It is difficult enough to justify your own embarkation on a journey with little certainty of ever reaching the destination, let alone to persuade fellow travellers to accompany you.

Contrary to commonly held doctrine, Sustainability as a rationale has been with us for a long time. In its simplest form, Sustainability refers to the ability of something to keep going *ad infinitum*. In times past this notion was essential to our day-to-day survival. Long distance transport and communication were arduous, consequentially exploitable resources were held at unnaturally finite levels. 'Good housekeeping' was a precondition to success (in the Darwinian sense of the word). It was very difficult to develop un-sustainably. In the last 250 years colonialism, industrialisation and globalisation have removed the need for restraint, as a result, development has advanced exponentially. In short, what we have witnessed over the last three centuries is the demise of *forced or imposed sustainability*.

Sustainable Development, a spin-off from the original concept of sustainability, is a late twentieth century phrase, rooted in centuries of conception. On 21 August 1910, Theodore Roosevelt, then President of the United States of America, delivered a speech to the people of Kansas City. In this speech, without using the title, he unintentionally outlined some of the key issues surrounding Sustainable Development: 'Conservation means development as much as it does protection. I recognise the right and duty of this generation to develop and use the natural resources of our land; but I do not recognise the right to waste them, or to rob, by wasteful use, the generations that come after us' (Boukhari, 2000; Dudley, 2003).

Implicit in this little-quoted paragraph, Roosevelt pre-empted the need to set 'limits to growth', that is, limits that respect society, our environment and intergenerational equity. 'Conservation', as he termed it, did not need to hinder development – rather, if used correctly, the two concepts could co-exist, complementing each other.

Unfortunately, few people heeded the advice of Roosevelt and over the following 50 years industrial development continued at a previously unparalleled rate. Little regard was paid to the environment, equity or society. In 1962 the ecologist Rachel Carson reawakened the debate by publishing her book 'Silent Spring' (Carson, 1962). In this bestseller she outlined the effects of insecticides and pesticides on songbird populations throughout the United States. This seemingly innocuous theme hit home, and invoked an outpouring of emotive indignation. The book is often credited with triggering much of the contemporary US environmental legislation – it certainly prompted a ban on DDT[7] – and galvanised the environmental movement.

Sustainability issues were given their next real airing by the *Club of Rome*[8] in 1972. Their landmark report *The Limits to Growth* contained 'a model built specifically to investigate five major trends of global concern – accelerating industrialisation, rapid population growth, widespread malnutrition, depletion of non-renewable resources, and a deteriorating environment' (Meadows, 1972). They concluded that:

Man possesses, for a small moment in his history, the most powerful combination of knowledge, tools, and resources the world has ever known. He has all that is physically necessary to create a totally new form of human society – one that would be built to last for generations. The two missing ingredients are a realistic, long-term goal that can guide mankind to the equilibrium society and the human will to achieve that goal. Without such a goal and a commitment to it, short-term concerns will generate the exponential growth that drives the world system toward the limits of the earth and ultimate collapse (Ibid).

The Club of Rome recommended immediate action to avert a global crisis. Time soon proved their model to be inaccurate, but interestingly and perhaps more importantly, the trends that they identified have not disappeared (see, The Club of Rome, 2003).

In 1979 Dr James Lovelock, then a National Aeronautics and Space Administration (NASA) scientist, added his contribution to the debate. His radically new scientific hypothesis proposed that the earth is a living, self-regulating system – acting like a giant organism (Lovelock, 1979). He suggested that organisms do not just adapt to the environment (the basis of Darwin's evolutionary theory), they also change it. According to Lovelock, all organisms on earth are intelligently self-regulating, with the obvious exception of humankind. Following this line of thought it becomes apparent that if 'all life' is potentially important to the well-being of the planet then it must all be conserved with greater care. Lovelock's hypothesis was in the public domain for a further eight years (in the mean time among other events, the Union Carbide chemical factory at Bhopal, India leaked a deadly gas immediately killing 3800 people; scientists discovered the Antarctic ozone hole; and the Russian nuclear reactor at Chernobyl exploded with catastrophic long-term consequences) before the global community eventually revisited sustainability, granting it the status and prominence that it deserved. In 1987 the World Commission on Environment and Development published *'Our Common Future'* (WCED, 1987) more commonly known as the *Brundtland Report*. In this report the WCED defined the phrase Sustainable Development, although many subsequent authors/organisations have constructed their own versions (see Table 2.1). This remains the pre-eminent and most frequently cited definition. Although it is a widely accepted definition, there is still little or no agreement about what it might mean in practical or theoretical terms.

Table 2.1 Key definitions of Sustainable Development

World Commission on Environment and Development (WCED)

Meeting the needs of the present without compromising the ability of future generations to meet their own needs. ... The process of change in which the expectation of resources, the direction of investments, the orientation of technological development, and institutional change are all in harmony and enhance both current and future potential to meet human needs and aspirations. (WCED, 1987)

World Business Council for Sustainable Development (WBCSD)

Forms of progress that meet the needs of the present without compromising the ability of future generations to meet their needs. (World Business Council for Sustainable Development, 2003)

The United Kingdom's Sustainable Development Strategy

Living on the earth's income rather than eroding its capital. It means keeping the consumption of renewable resources within the limits of their replenishment. It means handing down to successive generations not only man-made wealth, but also natural wealth, such as clean and adequate water supplies, good arable land, a wealth of wildlife, and ample forests.

The strategy has four key objectives:

Social progress which recognises the needs of everyone
Effective protection of the environment
Prudent use of natural resources
Maintenance of high and stable levels of economic growth and employment.

(HM Government, 1999)

World Conservation Union

Improving the quality of life while living within the carrying capacity of ecosystems. (Munro & Martin W Holdgate, 1991)

Forum for the Future

Sustainable Development is a dynamic process which enables all people to realise their potential, and to improve their quality of life, in ways which simultaneously protect and enhance the Earth's life support systems. (Forum for the Future, 2003)

Based on these established definitions it would seem that organisations committed to Sustainable Development[9] should be active in promoting the following five key themes:

1. intergenerational equity
2. protection, preservation and ideally improvement of the environment
3. continued economic growth
4. societal progress
5. global inclusiveness

These themes and the modern concept of Sustainable Development have evolved as the result of a compromise between two seemingly opposed agendas, those of the developed world and those of the developing world. In the past industrialised, developed countries tended to be chiefly concerned with environmental issues such as pollution and declining biodiversity, while their counterparts from developing countries were firmly focused on developmental issues. It was this ongoing debate that prevented the Rio Summit on Environment and Development (more commonly known as the Earth Summit) being called the Rio Summit on Sustainable Development. During the summit the concept of Sustainable Development was re-examined and clarified. Both developed and developing countries acknowledged that theoretically the concept would be mutually beneficial; it would promote significant economic development, without the costly environmental consequences that developed countries feared. In order to facilitate its global implementation the Summit witnessed the launch of a *UN* commission on Sustainable Development (UNCSD). In the spirit of Sustainable Development the Summit also witnessed the signing of Agenda 21,[10] the Convention on Biological Diversity (CBD) and the UN Framework Convention on Climate Change (UNFCCC). Following this, the September 2002 Johannesburg Summit (Rio + 10) was un-controversially titled the 'World summit on Sustainable Development'. Sustainable Development had fully entered the global lexicon. In the intervening period between Rio and Johannesburg, Sustainable Development became an explicit objective of the European Union (EU) (since the ratification of the *Amsterdam Treaty* in May 1999). Under the amended Article 2 of the treaty: 'The community shall have as its task ... to promote throughout the Community a harmonious, balanced and sustainable development of economic activities, sustainable and non-inflationary growth' (European Commission, 1999). This legal acknowledgement of Sustainable Development was proof of its emerging status, both as a universal responsibility and in the future as a necessary precursor to economic growth.

For the purposes of this study, I do not wish to add further to the swarm of definitions and I am happy to adopt the 1987 WCED classic text. With this hurdle removed, we are able to move forward and examine how its objectives can be implemented. Those authors and organisations still wrestling with definitions are finding that they are being overtaken by an issue driven agenda.

The implementation of Sustainable Development is a more controversial and genuine issue. As we have seen in the introduction, the global environmental and social situation is far from favourable. Lovins *et al.*, in their influential book *Factor Four*, highlight some of the difficulties associated with implementation and they suggest that to achieve sustainable development we will need to grow resource productivity fourfold: doubling wealth and simultaneously halving resource use (Lovins *et al.*, 1998). On the basis of this alone it would be fair to suggest that achieving sustainability will not be easy, and will certainly not be achieved by any individual government, company, or civil society organisation. If it were possible to unilaterally double wealth and half resource use one would have thought that more companies would be engaging. The reality is that companies have found that they can only advance the agenda by working in concert.

2.3.1 Partnerships: Moving forward in concert

I suggested earlier that Sustainable Development is a direction, a journey and not a destination. As with any journey it is safer and more effective to travel in groups, blazing a wide trail instead of having to negotiate small and dangerous paths. Sustainable Development could therefore be perceived as a societal challenge only 'achievable' through effective multi-stakeholder (governments, individuals, NGOs and corporations etc.) partnerships and coalitions (Tonn, 1999). Business engagement, contrary to the mantra of many NGOs, is not a panacea in itself. It is easy to pass the buck, but at the end of the day it is perfectly possible to argue that rampant Western societal consumption drives corporate growth in the first place.

In a recent report the World Business Council for Sustainable Development echoed this view, concluding that sustainability had to be achieved through the market, with all societal actors cooperating in what is by virtue a 'shared responsibility' (Holliday and Pepper, 2001).

Eighteen years on from the publication of *Our Common Future*, Sustainable Development has become a mainstream concern and issue for big business. This is poignantly exemplified by corporate attendance at World Summits. At the 1992 Rio summit on Environment and Development, business was underrepresented, while at the 2002 conference this situation was dramatically reversed: Business Action for Sustainable Development, an independent organisation that was setup specifically to put across the business perspective, managed to field more than 40 high profile CEOs and hundreds of other corporate representatives.

Corporate sustainability, in its various guises, now attracts regular attention (positive and negative) in 'hard-core' business journals such as the *Financial Times*, *Fortune Magazine*, *Harvard Business Review* and the

Economist – although it seems to attract more attention in Europe than in Asia or the United States.

In March 2001, *Fortune Magazine* quoted Pasquale Pistorio (CEO ST Microelectronics) as saying that 'Sustainability is not in contradiction with good financial return' (Muller, 2001). A recent study conducted by Graves and Waddock supported this view (Graves and Waddock, 2000). By studying the same group of companies identified by Collins and Porras in their renowned book *Built to Last* they concluded that high standards of responsibility directly impact long-term firm performance. In other words, outperforming their peers in terms of responsibility contributed towards the success of Collins and Porras's 'Visionary Companies'. The corporate 1980s were marked by the 'Quality Revolution' – Total Quality Management (TQM) that swept across all industries and sectors during the decade and is now considered standard practice – corporate sustainability could be set to represent the revolution of the twenty-first century. *Fortune* predicted this trend in as early as 1990. Then environmentalism was heralded as businesses 'New Crusade', (Kirkpatrick, 1990). The same article went further and stated that:

> The smartest companies are not just facing the music, they're singing along.

This statement could not have been closer to the truth. 'Smart companies' are trying to engage civil society, moving from being part of the problem to being part of the solution (the drivers for this change in behaviour are explored in section 2.5). As a result many companies are now working with the activists that they once fought. Co-operation, as opposed to confrontation is fostering an atmosphere of increased innovation and stimulating progress. In his best selling book of the same name Glen Peters calls this practice 'Waltzing with the Raptors' (Peters, 1999).

In the glossy world of PR it would seem that businesses have made a great deal of progress towards sustainability. However this is not the whole story. Despite superficial impressions, very few companies are moving forward in concert with other social actors. Many are stalled in confusion, unclear about their corporate obligations/responsibilities towards Sustainable Development. Indeed, many companies argue that they need not do anything about sustainability because that should be the exclusive role of government, this position is often inflamed by the frequent usage of the term responsibility.

Obviously, depending on an actor's position in society his/her contribution towards Sustainable Development will vary. The question as to what form the corporate contribution to Sustainable Development takes is a pertinent one. Stakeholders are being told that companies are committed to sustainability and/or accountability and/or social responsibility and/or being good citizens. But by openly using conflicting terminology companies are inadvertently furthering confusion. The following section aims to clarify corporate responsibility terminology and to investigate the corporate contribution to Sustainable Development.

2.4 The Tower of Babel: Corporate contributions

A number of business organisations, consultancies, think tanks, and academics have sought to establish what the concept of Sustainable Development means to business. This has resulted in the development of several models/frameworks/notions which corporations use (sometimes interchangeably, sometimes inconsistently) as the basis for their sustainability strategy. The five notions outlined in this section enjoy almost complete exclusivity in the field.

To give a very rough idea about the relative take-up of these notions I have performed an internet search on each of them (see Table 2.2). Using Boolean logic the phrase itself was placed within inverted commas and searched for using google.com – the internet's pre-eminent search engine:

Corporate Social Responsibility (CSR) and Corporate Citizenship (CC) are clearly the frontrunners; even accounting for error (which would be significant) in terms of popularity they are far ahead of the other notions. This should not come as a surprise, as a large number of

Table 2.2 Phrase search on Google.com

Notion	Approximate google.com search result on 6th May 2003. (Searching over 3 billion pages: Number of pages found).
'The triple bottom line'	11,200 or 27,200 [without 'The']
'The five capitals model'	31 or 46 [without 'The'] or 522 [without 'the and 'model']
'The natural step framework'	971 or 1,020 [without 'The']
'Corporate social responsibility'	151,000
'Corporate citizenship'	81,700

companies and organisations are using CSR and CC as overarching describers of the corporate commitment to Sustainable Development. 'The triple bottom line' (TBL), 'five capitals', and 'the natural step' are by nature more like frameworks, and therefore less likely to be quoted. It is also worth noting that the TBL is, to all intents and purposes, a proprietary framework (although not trademarked), held by the UK company SustainAbility; consequentially other companies refer to it differently.

2.4.1 The triple bottom line and its variants

Back in 1998 John Elkington, the chairman of progressive strategy consultancy SustainAbility, institutionalised the now famous concept of the TBL. In his book, *Cannibals with Forks: The Triple Bottom Line of 21st Century Business* (Elkington, 1998), he outlined how 21st century business would be increasingly called to demonstrate not only its financial, but also its social and environmental performance (see figure 2.2). He suggested that enhancing environmental quality and social equity are just as important for business as striving for profits.

On the SustainAbility website John Elkington uses a continental drift as an analogy to describe the TBL; he suggests that we should 'think of each bottom line as a continental plate, often moving independently from the others. As the plates move under, over or against each other, 'shear zones' emerge where the social, economic or ecological equivalents of tremors and earthquakes occur.' (SustainAbility Ltd, 2003).

'Three pronged' models of this nature have been talked about extensively since the publication of the *Brundtland Report*, although using a multitude of different analogies. Some practitioners refer to:

- The three legged stool or three pillars (see Figure 2.3). If one leg/pillar is missing, the stool/structure falls over. If one leg/pillar is too long or too short, the stool/structure is unstable;
- Pyramids (see Figure 2.1);
- Spheres, or the Russian Doll (see Figure 2.4);
- Or, Venn diagrams (see Figure 2.5).

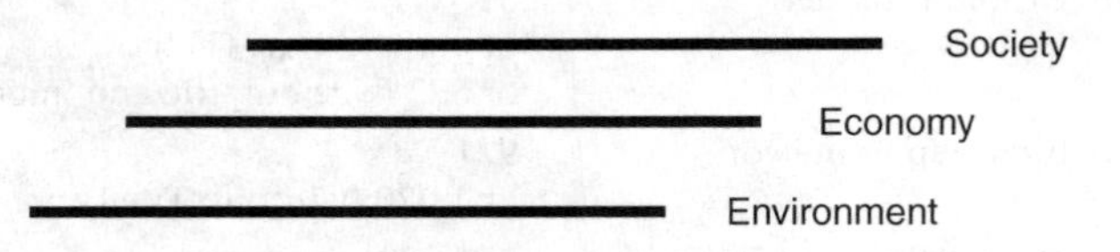

Figure 2.2 'The triple bottom line', adapted from figure on SustainAbility's website (SustainAbility Ltd, 2003).

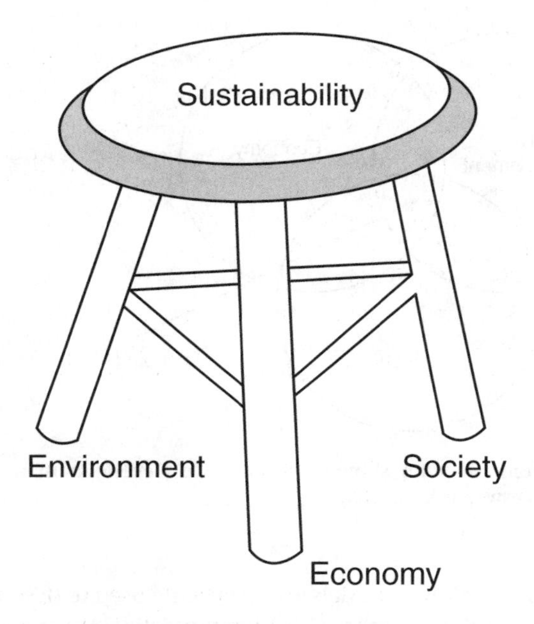

Figure 2.3 The three-legged stool of Sustainability.

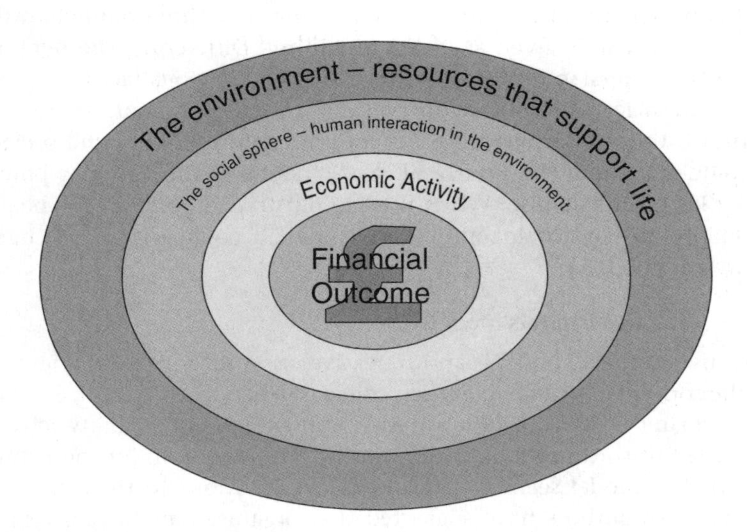

Figure 2.4 Spheres of Sustainability, from Sd3 Ltd (Sd3 Ltd, 2003).

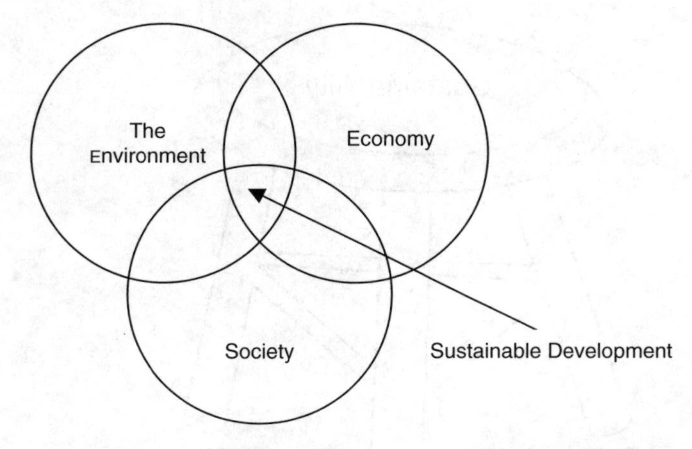

Figure 2.5 Venn diagram showing Sustainable Development as the point of convergence between three circles.

Metaphors aside, all five models are essentially used to describe the same thing albeit in different ways. This highly practical three-way model has been accepted by a large number of businesses, possibly due to its conceptual simplicity, and it now represents the basis of the current trend in sustainability reporting. It does, however, have a major problem: it does not consider any of the three lines as being more important than the other – the TBL is given an equal weighting. Differently, the pyramid and sphere/Russian doll models, recognise the obvious fact that economy and society cannot function without the environment, whereas, in contrast, the environment can function without economy and society. I would argue that the overtly simplistic nature of the TBL may potentially lead to its demise. When used to illustrate a point in the boardroom or office of sustainability sceptics the TBL could arguably do harm as well as good.

2.4.2 The five capitals model

The 'five capitals' model is an innovative, asset management approach to the concept of sustainability accredited independently to both Stephan Viederman (Viederman, 1996) an American author/sustainability activist, and the British think-tank Forum for the Future (Forum for the Future, 2003). The model seeks to pare down organisations to their essential assets. Both authors have suggested that organisations have access to five forms of capital, all of which, if un-degraded, will generate a return.

Table 2.3 Forum for the Future's 'five capitals' and 'twelve features', adapted from their website (Forum for the Future, 2003)

Forum for the Future's 'five capitals'
1. natural Capital, e.g. resources, sinks and processes
2. human Capital, e.g. knowledge, values, health
3. social Capital, e.g. families, communities, businesses, culture, schools
4. manufactured Capital, e.g. tools, machines, infrastructure, buildings
5. financial Capital, e.g. shares, bonds or banknotes

The models differ slightly, the primary difference being Forum for the Future's inclusion of 'Financial Capital' at the expense of Viederman's 'Cultural Capital' – which is considered to be already represented under social capital.

The Forum's thesis suggests that 'by maintaining and trying to increase stocks of these capital assets, we can live off the income, without reducing the capital itself. But for this to happen it is the responsibility of every organisation, business or otherwise, to manage these capital assets sustainably' (Forum for the Future, 2003).

Following this model a 'sustainable business' would appear to be one that adds to the capital worth of each of the five capitals – at the very least not causing significant erosion to any of the five capitals at the expense of others. The business would simply live off the interest that well managed capital provides. The model is not solely directed at business and could easily be used to develop national frameworks for sustainability. Despite this a number of, primarily British, companies have subscribed to its perspective, Wessex Water PLC being one of the most vocal supporters. In a notable development, the 'five capitals' was adopted as the basis of a set of new holistic sustainability management guidelines: *The SIGMA Project* was developed as a government funded partnership between the British Standards Institute, Forum for the Future and AccountAbility.[11] In late 2005 the British Standards Institute will publish a further incarnation of the SIGMA guidelines: BS 8900. 'BS 8900 Guidelines for Sustainability Management' also look set to incorporate the 'five capitals' approach.

2.4.3 The natural step framework

The Natural Step[12] was founded in 1989 by Dr Karl-Henrik Robèrt, then a Swedish oncologist. Whilst performing cancer research he identified a significant increase in childhood leukaemia cases. Further investigation suggested that this was linked to the presence of toxins at a cellular level–preventing normal cellular function. Dr Robèrt linked his observations to the bigger picture, noticing that in general, as our environment degraded, so did our health. In doing so, he observed that the contemporary ecological debate tended to be focused on prevention and not on cure. Together with 50 other Swedish scientists he set out to apply 'systems thinking' (recognising that what happens to one part of a system ultimately affects every other part) to our understanding of the biosphere's functions and societies' impact on them. In essence, Robèrt and his team were expanding on the earlier work of Lovelock – building a Gaiaean type framework for the implementation of sustainability in organisations. The conclusions of their research were considered to be so important that every household and school in Sweden received a copy. Dr Robèrt, working with another scientist, the physicist John Holmberg, followed up this research by defining a set of four system conditions for sustainability (Robèrt, 2002). They proposed that a sustainable society, organisation or business should have as their objective the realisation of these conditions – balancing supply and demand.

In a sustainable society, nature is not subject to systematically increasing:

1. concentrations of substances extracted from the earth's crust
2. concentrations of substances produced by society
3. degradation by physical means; and, that in society
4. human needs are met worldwide

'The natural step framework' acknowledges that change is a gradual process, and advocates a step by step, targets-based, approach. As a result their organisation promotes business take-up of initiatives like EMAS,[13] ISO 14001[14] and life cycle analysis (Robèrt *et al.*, 2002). 'The natural step framework' is commonly put into perspective using a funnel diagram. The diagram suggests that with time, society will place increasing demands on the environment at the same time as resources are in decline. Robèrt suggests that companies risk hitting the walls of the funnel (going out of business) if they do not strive to meet the four system conditions.

By concentrating on cause rather than effect Robèrt has devised an easily understandable, scientifically grounded, methodology to guide society and organisations towards sustainability.

His original idea is now common knowledge in his native Sweden and has since been adopted by over 70 MNCs worldwide including most recently: The Bank of America, McDonald's, Home Depot, Interface,

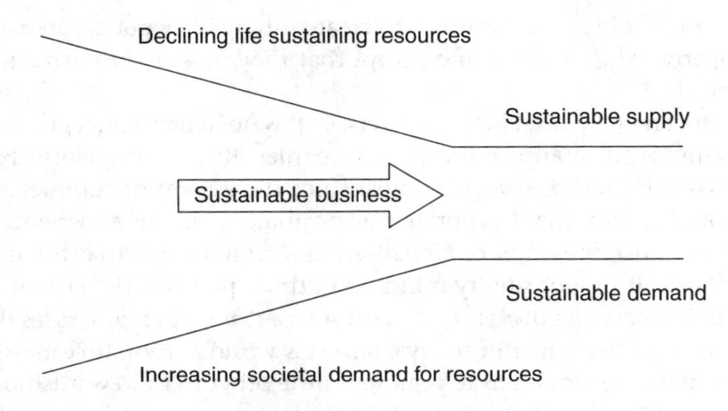

Figure 2.6 'The natural step' funnel, adapted from (Robert, 2002).

Starbucks, Nike and IKEA. These businesses have adopted the framework as a planning tool, enabling the integration of sustainability considerations into the corporate decision making process.

2.4.4 Corporate Social Responsibility

Corporate Social Responsibility, or CSR as it is more commonly know, is certainly the most prominent of the five concepts outlined here. Despite this there is little standardisation with respect to its usage. As a result it seems to mean all things to all people.

The phrase controversially suggests that a company has a responsibility to someone other than its owners (i.e. shareholders). This concept is most prominently opposed by the Milton Friedman type ideology; Friedman has suggested that only individuals can have a responsibility, the corporation as an artificial person can only have artificial responsibilities. Friedman termed CSR a 'fundamentally subversive doctrine in a free society', and went on to propose that in such a society, 'there is one and only one social responsibility of business – to use its resources and engage in activities designed to increase its profits so long as it stays within the rules of the game, which is to say, engages in open and free competition without deception or fraud' (Friedman, 1963). Sternberg (1998) builds on this philosophy, suggesting that companies advocating a stakeholder approach (fundamental to CSR) are depriving stockholders of their property rights. Baker responds to this, reminding us that in today's business climate the 'property value' of a company is far exceeded by its market capitalisation (Baker, 2003). It would seem that if stockholders wish to capitalise on some of the benefits that globalisation brings (primarily an opportunity to create intangible value far in excess of property value) they should accept that they must relinquish a level of control.

Despite Friedman and his supporters, CSR is not a new concept – it has been around for many centuries. Companies all over the world have practised this kind of strategy almost since the advent of commerce. If anything I suggest that Corporate Responsibility (CR) has experienced a downturn since the onset of globalisation. I would argue that the main reason for this 'responsibility mindset' in times past was the lack of differentiation between owners and managers of firms – in many cases they were one and the same. In today's business world corporate leadership of quoted companies tends to represent little other than stewardship for a short period of time. Prominent historical examples of best practice include: Cadbury's, Lever Brothers, Toyota and FIAT.[15] These Companies (primarily through their leadership) felt that they had a responsibility to their local community, and consequentially invested heavily in it (controversy was avoided because their company's money was in fact their own); CSR has historically been local. This local tradition continues to date, in America. Corning, Deere, Wal-Mart, Maytag and Smithfield are just a few of the many examples of Fortune 500 companies that still maintain what are often called 'company towns'. Following this, it could certainly be argued that 'original' CSR translates too little other than enlightened self-interest.[16] The challenge for CSR as we enter the twenty-first century appears to be whether it can move from local to global. To do so it will require a radical rethink of the underlying philosophy – or perhaps a new concept altogether.

Although CSR, in itself, is not a model, it is outlined here because it is the most commonly misused concept. Currently, a number of media sources, organisations and a handful of prominent companies are using CSR as an overarching expression for the net contribution of business to Sustainable Development. This usage is unhelpful (bearing in mind the historical context) and misplaced, as Figure 2.7 shows, CSR is quite simply the social strand of a 'three pronged' sustainability strategy. CSR is authoritatively defined as 'the commitment of business to contribute to sustainable economic development, working with employees, their families, the local community and society at large to improve their quality of life' (Watts and Holme, 2000). It is not useful to use CSR to refer to the net contribution of business to Sustainable Development because it implies that the only reason we would conserve or protect the environment is because society demands it. The phrase suggests that environment, *per se,* does not have its own innate value. This goes against the

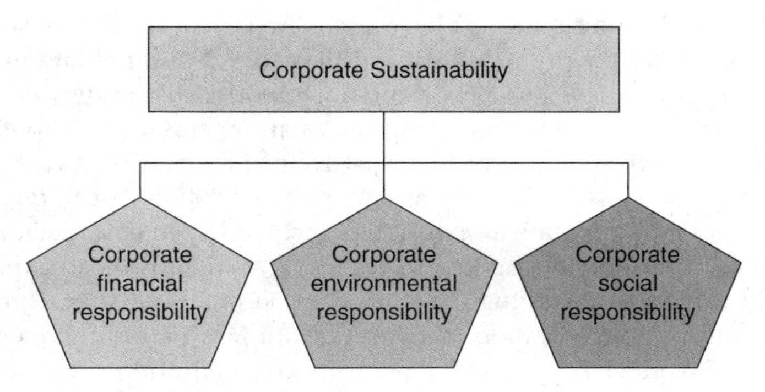

Figure 2.7 The de-construction of CSR – adapted from (Watts and Holme, 1999).

founding ethos of Sustainable Development, according to which companies have a responsibility to reduce much more than just their impact on society; they must champion causes that are seemingly silent – such as the environment, future generations, and the like.

In the United States CSR has been traditionally used to refer to companies' philanthropy strategies, that is, the distribution of a certain percentage of profits to charities. In fact, philanthropy is still the basis of many American companies' CSR strategy (see Porter and Kramer, 2002; Smith, 1994). The theory being that this is the best way (aside from taxation) they can give back to society some of what they have taken. No one would deny that giving money to charity is a good thing – in fact, the more the better. But it is debatable if this is really the most effective/efficient way to spend money if your ultimate objective is societal or environmental improvement. To draw an analogy, this policy is similar in nature to 'end of pipe' environmental solutions and consequently has the same drawbacks. It would seem that it would be far more advisable for a company to examine its own societal footprint[17] – by striving to reduce the negative implications of this footprint it is likely that a company can have a greater positive impact on society.

Within the EU the concept of CSR has attracted much attention; in 2001 the European Commission responded to this enhanced attention by publishing a Green Paper outlining a European framework for responsibility (European Commission Directorate-General for Employment and Social Affairs, 2001). This report presented a rather confused picture. Only two years earlier the EU had whole-heartedly committed to the concept of Sustainable Development – as institutionalised in its fifth and sixth action plans – and the Green Paper did little, or nothing, to link CSR to this objective. As I have argued so far, in theory CSR should not be used to refer to the holistic business contribution to Sustainable Development – as the European Commission originally proposed.

One way to get around this obstacle, as an organisation, is to either clarify your own meaning of CSR, that is, in the majority of cases CSR refers equally to environmental and social responsibility, or to rephrase CSR as simply 'Corporate Responsibility'; which would be a much fairer and more appropriate description. Waddock *et al.*, provide an explanation of this term suggesting that Corporate Responsibility refers to the 'recognition and integration of Triple Bottom Line performance expectations' (Waddock *et al.*, 2002). Following this definition, CSR – or CR can be finally linked with Sustainable Development. But this only removes part of the problem, the use of the term 'responsibility' means that CR will be unlikely to enter the mainstream business lexicon – certainly while limited liability legislation governs corporations.

I believe that corporations should have a responsibility to society and to the environment, if I were a CEO I would consider this as one of my mandates. However not all business people share my outlook on life. In fact they often confuse the enthusiasm for responsibility with the business case for sustainability, as a result they reject both. As I will argue in this book it is perfectly plausible, if you are not so inclined, to take one and not the other. Businesses may engage in sustainability on its own without accepting the seemingly liberal agenda that comes together with CSR.

Summarising, CSR represents an effective way for companies to reduce their impact on society, perhaps securing their theoretical licence to operate. It should certainly generate a much needed feedback mechanism between companies and their stakeholders – building trust. The primary arguments against theoretical CSR are flawed because they are grounded in the 1960s economic and socio-political landscape influenced by Friedman and do little to take into account recent changes resulting from the onset and domination of globalisation. It seems unlikely that CSR as a concept will ever have an explicit definition; global economic, social and environmental conditions are in a constant state of flux and as a result CSR is constantly evolving to meet this changing agenda. However as CSR evolves, its name and historical context prevents it from representing a holistic approach to sustainability – indeed, if a company is pursuing social responsibility it could be accused of being irresponsible with regard to its environmental and financial obligations. Equally, the use of the term 'responsibility' has the effect of removing the corporate focus from 'opportunity' and 'risk' and on to obligation. I would suggest that opportunity and risk are likely to represent greater drivers for change. Despite this, ultimately we could conclude that it is the outcome that is important, not the process, and CSR is certainly currently producing positive societal and environmental outcomes.

2.4.5 Corporate citizenship

The recent global corporate citizenship (CC) debate has been primarily driven by the efforts of several key people and their institutions, Sandra Waddock of Boston College, Simon Zadek of AccountAbility and Malcolm McIntosh an independent consultant and teacher (Andriof and McIntosh, 2001; McIntosh *et al.*, 1998; Waddock, 2001; Zadek, 2001). The concept builds on the well-developed sociological theory of 'citizenship' and is not necessarily directly linked with Sustainable Development.

2.4.5.1 Citizenship

To aid our understanding of the terms, and to ensure correct usage, I believe that it is important first to look at its derivation. The concept of citizenship appears to have two primary roots, first the Aristotelian definition, and second the Florentine interpretation. It is important to note that the concept is historically only applied to the individual and is closely intertwined with republicanism.

Aristotle famously suggested that man is by nature a political or social animal (zoon politikon, see Barker, 1948). In order to fulfil his potential, Aristotle argued that man needs to live within a political community. Within this community man as a citizen, should work towards justice and common good, peace and prosperity. This is often called the 'civic republican tradition', a direct democracy where all citizens take part in political decisions. Within Renaissance Italy all citizens were equal under the law, even if one was wealthier than the other. Citizens were able to benefit from certain rights, but in return they were obliged to take an unpaid interest in politics and defend the republic when required. Writing in more recent times, David Held suggests that 'Citizenship has meant a reciprocity of rights against, and duties towards, the community. Citizenship has entailed membership, membership of the community in which one lives one's life. And membership has invariably involved degrees of participation in the community' (Held, 1991). Following this, we could conclude that contemporary citizenship involves acting responsibility as an equal member within a particular community.

2.4.5.2 Corporations as citizens

Now the question is: Is it possible for corporations to behave as citizens, within the restraints of this essentially social concept? Based purely on a theoretical background, it seems obvious that corporations, as assemblages of citizens, cannot be citizens in their own right. They could however strive to behave in a manner which befits a citizen. Following the earlier description of 'citizenship', it appears that one of the most central aspects of theoretical citizenship is the 'community of belonging'. Before we ask multinationals to act like citizens we must ask ourselves what community it is that they belong to – in the aftermath of extensive globalisation perhaps it is an extension of Habermas's hotly contested 'public sphere' (Habermas, 1964).

How does a company that aspires to become a responsible citizen determine what it is that society considers to be 'responsible behaviour'? The emerging answer is relatively simple, they must ask society (even if we consider the environment as a stakeholder, it has no voice). Companies have to first determine and then engage their stakeholders. McIntosh *et al.*, concur with this, pointing out that CC 'suggests a two-way relationship between society and corporations' (McIntosh *et al.*, 1998). It is only by engaging all those who affect or are affected by the organisation (Freeman, 1984), that business can determine the acceptable or appropriate course of action. This engagement generally takes the form of a 'virtuous responsibility circle' (see Figure 2.8), whereby stakeholders are engaged in a permanent cyclical dialogue process, the outcome of which is a form of behaviour that conforms to societal demands (Brady, 2002, 2003).

McIntosh et al., suggest that progress towards CC is taking place along a continuum, the first stage being 'minimalist', whereby corporations simply comply with legislation, the second stage is 'discretionary', that is, corporations engage society by the donation of money (philanthropy); the third, and final stage is 'Strategic', whereby citizenship is fully integrated into business (McIntosh *et al.*, 1998).

Thus what is the contribution of CC to sustainability? I argue that CC could make a significant contribution, but again (for the same reasons as CSR) its application does not represent a holistic approach. As Waddock suggests, CC is 'the way a company integrates basic social values with everyday business practices, operations and policies (Boston College, 2003)'. It is for this reason that a number of companies operate a sustainability strategy in parallel with a CC programme, although behaving in a manner befitting a responsible citizen will certainly contribute towards sustainability. As an example Baxter Healthcare Inc. incorporates its

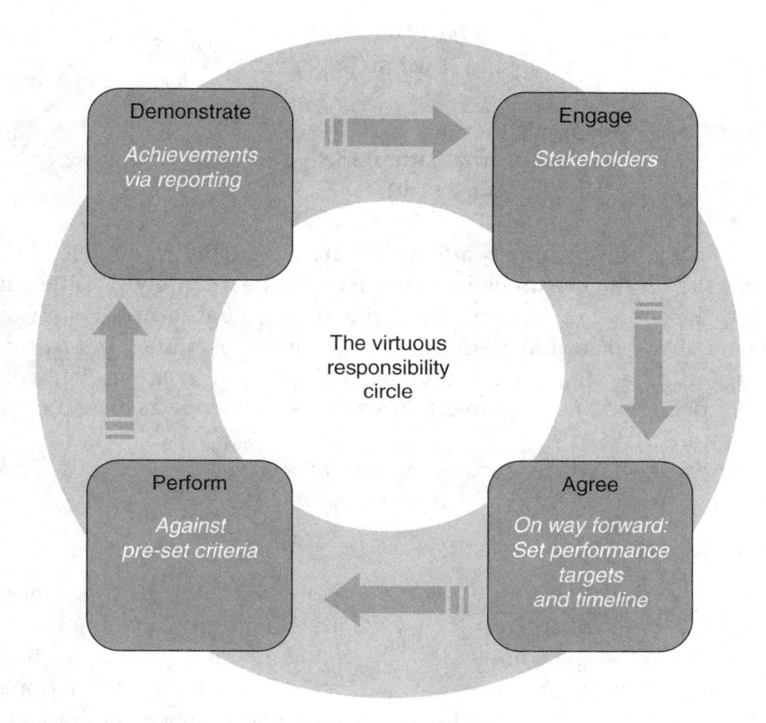

Figure 2.8 The virtuous responsibility circle.

objective to become a 'Best Citizen' (within all the communities that it operates), within the overall objective of Sustainable Development (Baxter International Inc, 2001).

Summarising, it would seem that CC is not, as some suggest, necessarily about 'companies taking into account their complete impact on society and the environment' (Roberts *et al.*, 2002), it's about companies acknowledging that they have a duty to act responsibly within the community, conforming to societal norms and responding to societal concerns – whatever these may be. On this basis it would seem that CC (like CSR), refers primarily to the social strand of Sustainable Development; crucially, societal concerns may not call for a level of change required to meet the Sustainable Development agenda.

2.5 Change drivers

Leaving aside the models, in terms of sustainable behaviour it would appear that there are things that MNCs *must do*, that is, they have an obligation; things that they *should do*, but don't always; and things that they *could do*, if they thought it would pay dividends.

1. The 'must' argument (the stick).
2. The 'should' argument (the natural inclination).
3. The 'could' argument (the carrot).

The 'could' and 'should' arguments are essentially intangible. As a result, their influence on behaviour is likely to be intensely variable and highly dependant on the individual organisation concerned. Following this variability, it would seem that it is the mindset, values and culture of organisations that determines whether these factors are individually influential. The 'must' argument, in stark contrast, appears to be universally influential.

In the following three sections each of these drivers are expanded on, detailing the commonly cited arguments for each.

2.5.1 Must

MNCs, by definition, operate trans-nationally. Whilst this brings obvious benefits for the company concerned it also brings a number of issues related to legal compliance. The company 'must' comply with all relevant laws in the countries of operation. National and international legislation aimed at limiting the socially unacceptable behaviour of corporates is increasing in volume on a daily basis. This is particularly true of environmental legislation within developed countries. The more the company expands, the more it must be aware of these differing and increasingly stringent, legal requirements. To reduce expenditure and risk of potential liability, for example, business often finds it easier to work to the highest common denominator within its sphere of operation. Although this is the most advisable[18] course of action it is of course by no means the standard. A number of companies try to avoid stringent legal obligations by transferring their operations overseas, to a nation with non-existent or lower regulation. The product or service is then exported to its chosen marketplace where it is sold at a lower price than is changed by competitors. The lower price being, in part, derived from the legal compliance cost savings.

Corporate avoidance of legislation is not however universal; indeed some companies are arguing for the global imposition of a level playing field. For example Phil Knight, Chairman and CEO of Nike, is quoted as saying 'We believe in a global system that measures *every* multinational against a *core set of universal standards* using an independent process of social performance monitoring akin to financial auditing' (in Zadek, 2001).

Legislative compliance is a unique driver in that it is non-discriminatory. Short of moving operations to a different country, it is difficult (read *costly*) to avoid. Companies, whether leaders or laggards, are forced to adopt more stringent responsibility guidelines. Increases in legislative volume are usually contested by companies, even leaders do not accept tighter rules easily. Contrary to the Nike stance, some companies claim that the free market will punish laggards of its own accord while at the same time offering leaders exclusive competitive advantage.[19] It is argued that this competitive advantage is eroded by the imposition of unavoidable guidelines.[20]

Despite this corporate dislike of legislation, it remains an effective tool to change corporate behaviour. This was exemplified recently in the US. The state of California, differently to other States, is able to set its own emissions standards. This is due to the geographical position of the Los Angeles basin which makes it historically vulnerable to acute air pollution. In July 2002 the California Governor, Grey Davis, enacted Assembly Bill 1493 (AB 1493), a statute directing the California Air Resources Board (CARB) to 'develop regulations to achieve maximum feasible cost-effective reductions in greenhouse gas emissions from new gasoline cars and light duty trucks vehicles, beginning in 2009' (California Air Resources Board, 2003). This unilateral action by the state of California has resulted in far reaching consequences for automotive companies wanting to trade there. First, through the Zero Emissions Vehicles mandate (ZEV) they were already required to produce clean, pollution-free vehicles as a percentage of their fleets (10 per cent by 2003); AB 1493 went one step further. If companies did not comply, then they would be refused permission to trade in the state of California. Through their business association, the American Automobile Manufacturers Association, automotive companies put up a sustained fight but were eventually defeated.

The California vehicle market is not particularly big when compared with the rest of the world, but it is nevertheless significant (as the largest in the US) and prestigious. Automotive companies who wanted a part of this market had no option but to adopt the legislation, absorbing any costs along the way. Ultimately, automotive companies have been forced to produce 'cleaner cars' (to the California standard) and then rather than incurring further costs (through having two types of each model) sell them nationwide. Companies that are able to meet the legislation first, stand to gain the most. For example, Toyota managed to mass-produce large numbers of its now-award-winning[21] hybrid car *Prius* within a short period of time. A number of other states are considering implementing AB 1493 (California Energy Commission, 2002): under a special provision of the Clean Air Act, any state is free to adopt the tougher measures in place of weaker federal rules. Back in California it remains to be seen how the new republican governor, Arnold Schwarzenegger, will respond to this legislation enacted by his predecessor; it is unlikely that he will dismiss it outright. To prop-up his green credentials he has already persuaded General Motors to custom manufacture a Hummer to run on hydrogen (his own Hummer was quoted as delivering just 11 miles per gallon), so perhaps the optimist can take a glimmer of hope.

There is no doubt that this stringent legislation has stimulated investment by global automotive manufactures in previously underfunded alternative fuel technologies. There are also far more fuel efficient cars on the streets of California, dramatically improving local air quality, and reducing overall $C0_2$ emissions. In 1980, the region had 101 Stage 1 smog alerts, while since 1999 (when the ZEV mandate was signed) it has had a total of zero (California Air Resources Board, 2003). Cairncross supported this example, pointing out that often companies can improve their environmental performance at little or no cost (Cairncross, 1991). However, the substantial improvements (of the nature required to achieve sustainability) cost real money. In these cases, practice would suggest that government needs to take an interventionist stance and tilt the playing field.

We can therefore conclude that legislative compliance is an effective driver of responsible behaviour, having an impact both in the country of operation/manufacture and (as we have seen in the California case) in the marketplace – a view echoed by some multinationals. It is unlikely however that legislation on its own will instigate the paradigm change that is necessary for the delivery of Sustainable Development. Throughout history paradigm changes (of the magnitude required), such as the first industrial revolution, have been delivered by market forces. Following this train of thought, I argue that legislation could act as a stimulus to innovation, tilting the playing field, and subsequently allowing market forces to take over.

2.5.2 Should

We are aware that as individuals we all have a degree of morality, indeed some would argue that it has a biological basis (Wilson, 1998). It is this morality that 'should' result in ethical behaviour. The important question is whether this morality can transgress the individual and seat itself in an organisation's psyche.

The answer is probably 'yes, it should do', but it is a *qualified* yes. After all, an organisation is little other than a group of individuals united by a common purpose. Its morality, or lack of it, can be determined by an examination of its purpose – in the case of corporations this purpose is usually enshrined in a mission or statement of values. This is something that all companies tend to have, the problem being that not all companies 'walk the talk'. To use the example of Enron, an examination of their mission/values would have revealed best practice; however events prove that reality on the ground was far from this. 'Moral' individuals had conspired to act immorally. We must take care not to tar all employees of Enron with the same brush, they were not all immoral. However, the case proves that for a firm to act immorally it only takes immoral leadership.

In the preface to her book *Costing the Earth* Cairncross cites peer pressure as a primary driver of moral behaviour. Interestingly, she suggests that pressure exerted by executive's children can represent a major force for change and the adoption of more environmentally friendly corporate practices. Added to this, she suggests that younger managers are more susceptible to societal pressures – and are therefore more anxious to do right by the environment (Cairncross, 1991).

It is possible to argue that 'limited liability' legislation, existing in most of the developed world (designed to protect shareholders from the actions of their company), represents an obstacle to a communal sense of morality. It states that a company is a separate legal entity, distinct from its owners, and they are not personally liable for the actions of the company. It has the unfortunate side effect of sending the signal to corporate leadership that their 'owners' do not care about the state of their property – provided the share price rises.

Even if we assume that organisations 'can' act as morally responsible units, the question of 'whose morals' then arises. To exemplify this, we should take a look at the issue of child labour. To me, my colleagues and most of the developed world, child labour is immoral, and quite simply unacceptable. However, in certain countries in the developing world it is not only morally acceptable, but also economically speaking, it is one of the lynchpins of family life (see Bachman, 2000). A recent UNICEF study found that many families in India were 'dependent on it for sustaining the household at near subsistence levels' (Chandrasekhar, 2002). As a result of this situation, when multinationals inform their suppliers in developing countries of the need to prevent child labour, resentment and confusion could arise.

So, is there a moral case for corporate responsibility? Yes, certainly, but it is not something to be relied upon. Even 'alleged' moral individuals act immorally from time to time. This is why societies have constructed constitutions (in some cases), laws and criminal justice systems. If individuals cannot be completely trusted to act in a moral way, it is probably unwise to suggest that companies, run by individuals, will all be empowered by morality as a driver of responsibility.

2.5.3 Could: Competitive advantage

Few businesses or business leaders would today deny the fact that responsibility 'could' offer some form of competitive advantage. Indeed the implementation of 'eco-efficiency' measures has been proven to offer considerable and, more importantly, tangible cost advantages. But this is not revolutionary thinking. The 1996 catchphrase of Womack and Jones' famous book, *Lean Thinking* was: 'Banish Waste and Create Wealth in Your Corporation' (Womack and Jones, 1996); and even then much of the research was based on pre-existing Japanese manufacturing techniques. 'Smart' companies should have been practicing this technique for at least the past six or seven years.

To decide on the viability of responsibility programmes, most companies employ simple, time-honoured, cost-benefit analysis (CBA) techniques. This is likely to be the primary reason that the majority of companies find it difficult to move beyond eco-efficiency.

Obviously, if one tries to compute traditional economic metrics (financials) with intangibles, a by-product of an increasingly globalised economy, one will not receive a helpful answer. This should not come as a surprise, for we were all taught at primary school that you cannot add apples and pears. The findings of an exercise of this nature will certainly not support the theory that responsibility could deliver competitive advantage. Allen Greenspan, Chairman of the United States Federal Reserve, went some way to acknowledging the importance of intangibles in a speech entitled 'Maintaining Economic Vitality', given at Grand Falls, Michigan in 1999. He asserted that: 'Most of what we currently perceive as value and wealth is intellectual and impalpable' (Federal Reserve Board, 1999). If most of what we consider as wealth and value is impalpable then companies should surely reconsider the method and information that they use to compute their CBA? This situation is grounded in a major flaw in neo-classical economic thought (David Pearce *et al.*, 1989; Hardin, 1968; John Foster, 1997; Hawken *et al.*, 2000). The majority of environmental resources, despite in many cases being irreplaceable, are not assigned a realistic, if any, value. If they were then there would be no doubt that responsible usage of environmental resources was the way forward. For example, it costs companies vast sums of money to extract irreplaceable oil from the ground to provide us with energy, yet each day the sun provides us with heat and light – both of whose supply is secure, infinite and geographically well dispersed. The excuse given is that it costs too much to harness this type of energy, yet as any technologist will tell us, new technology always initially costs more. The more it is produced, the cheaper it becomes. Even the World Bank acknowledges that by using environmental economic techniques 'the wider array of benefits and costs associated with a project can be considered in deciding which alternative produces the largest net benefit to society' (World Bank, 2003).

As Oscar Wilde famously asserted 'it is a cynical man who knows the price of everything and the value of nothing'. It would seem that we have learned little since Garrett Hardin first outlined the *Tragedy of the Commons* in 1968 (Hardin, 1968). Global inequity is more pronounced than ever, population continues to grow at an unprecedented rate, and our common resources are still primarily held and used/consumed by the few. Through the prevalence of the *new medias* society is becoming increasingly aware that this situation is unsustainable. As a result, those companies that actively buck this trend and contribute to societies' collective goals could potentially extract advantage.

2.5.3.1 Societal compliance

Our ability to form functioning societies was something that many centuries ago began to distinguish our ancestors from their more primitive contemporaries. As our ancestors populated the globe, their societies developed. Collective action resulting from strong bonds, solidarity and human relationships were essential for and facilitated the development of better living standards and knowledge. Our ancestors had discovered that by working in groups it was significantly easier to achieve communal aims. The development of clans, or societies[22] also resulted in the delineation (territorial organisation) of the globe and the establishment of clear social and territorial borders. For centuries, wars were fought, territories were won and lost, and borders continuously re-invented. This process came to a head in the aftermath of the Second World War with the erection of the Iron Curtain between East and West, effectively dividing the globe into two clear factions – prevented from war-mongering by arguably the most dangerous product of collective action, the nuclear bomb.

We can see that in recent history societies had grown so much that individual linkages/communications between people, the foundation of a traditional society, were eroded and the groups acted in line with the wishes of increasingly powerful leaderships. We could assert that the twentieth century was defined by 'Big Government' (phrase, made famous by President Reagan used to describe an increased centralisation of power) and 'Big Companies'. At the close of the twentieth century this 'big is best' mentality was working. Companies acquired and merged at a ferocious pace. Stakeholders with concerns about CR were isolated and impotent, unable to use their strength in numbers. Union power was diminishing on a daily basis and the ability of individuals to collaborate was restricted due to under-developed communications. By being so big, these institutions/organisations were unintentionally alienating the very people they were originally designed to serve (for governments this means the electorate, for companies their customers, investors and employees[23]). Stakeholders became increasingly frustrated; unable to understand how something so big could ever listen or respond to their demands. Multinational corporations had become 'behemoths'.[24]

Although the size issue remains, the relationship between individuals and societies is rapidly evolving: modern communications have resulted in a reversal of a centuries old trend.[25] The Iron Curtain has fallen, globalisation, the increasing role of the internet and the 'CNN world' have together created a 'global goldfish bowl'. In response to this enhanced transparency and a growing global awareness of the issues and threats, corporations and governments alike are coming under intense pressure to change the way that they operate. As hiding places become few and far between, corporations need to become more responsive, to more people and quicker. It is important to note that 'Global corporations did not wake up one morning and decide to become socially responsible citizens, however. They were instead awakened, sometimes roughly, by the concerted efforts of civil society organisations' (Oliviero and Simmons, 2002). Today's stakeholders have 'found a voice', a powerful outlet for their corporate responsibility arguments (the new medias). Moreover, through this new outlet they have found strength in numbers (the initial reason for forming societies) and, implicitly, a propaganda machine capable of impacting corporate profitability. As the majority of sustainability issues are transboundary (i.e. child labour, air pollution, etc.) the pressure for change is greater on institutions that have a global scope/outlook. This became obvious in Seattle, Prague and Genoa (and many protests since) where large numbers of incensed protesters ('anti-globalisation' or 'no-global' groups) gathered to protest against the supposed arrogance and poor transparency of both the World Trade Organisation (WTO) and multinational corporations.

In this new, increasingly transparent environment many have argued that to operate efficiently a company must obtain 'societies' licence' (Business Action for Sustainable Development, 2003; Graafland, 2002; Massie, 2001; Post, 2002; Willums, 1998). Society has come to the realisation that business is built on the foundation of society (a stable version of which is required for growth), which is in turn rooted in the environment (the lowest common denominator). If business is to use the environment, it must first seek permission from its guardian – societies, who are looking after it for future generations. Business must prove that it is building intergenerational equity, not simply eroding it.

This is not a formal licence, it is a bond of trust between business and its stakeholders. If the bond of trust is broken, or worse still never constructed, the licence will be revoked and the company punished. This punishment commonly takes the form of negative propaganda, eroding reputational capital and brand value. The punishment being dealt out by a new generation of civil society organisations (more commonly known as Non-Governmental Organisations, NGOs), made powerful through their global reach and mastery of the 'new medias'.

In its 2002–03 issue, the *Yearbook of International Organizations* recognised some 38,000 international NGOs – more than five times as many as just 10 years ago. These organisations are active in nearly 300 countries and territories in the world today (Union of International Associations, 2002–03). There are approximately 60,000 MNCs (with a clear 'for profit' status) operating in the world, their presence is offset by almost 40,000 internationally active[26] civil society organisations, at a ratio of 1.5 to 1. When compared with civilian policing, for example, the problem that corporates face becomes clear; in London the Metropolitan Police operate at a ratio of 1 officer per 285 people (Johnston, 2001). Although not all NGOs are designed to police corporate behaviour – they are all civil society organisations with clearly defined societal goals.

Despite this high ratio, it is not unheard of for NGOs to make mistakes, the most obvious, high profile one being Greenpeace's mistaken positioning in the Brent Spar debacle.[27] Although most would agree that it is important to hold corporations to account for their activities, many argue that NGOs are impinging on the role of government, and quite fairly ask 'who guards the guards'? Most NGOs, despite primarily acting for the good of society, are non-elected, non-accountable organisations with un-transparent income streams. In fact, many are funded by wealthy corporate foundations. As international NGOs grow in size and influence we should soon expect to see them being called to establish their credentials upfront and verify their own accountability.

To conclude, at the beginning of the twenty-first century corporations are seriously vexed by NGOs. Most are aware of the damage that they can inflict, and actively try to avoid confrontation. Glen Peters, a management author, has drawn the comparison between NGOs and Velociraptors, one of the most ferocious predators ever to walk the earth. He suggests that it is not advisable for companies to attempt to outrun, or outwit the predators, instead he advises engagement. 'Imagine a different world ... Instead of trying to outwit it or keep it penned in some high voltage Jurassic Park, you find out why it wants to attack you' (Peters, 1999). He calls this process, 'dancing with the raptors'. While I accept the point that he makes, it is difficult to imagine that a Velociraptor would actually be dissuaded from eating something by 'engaging' with it. Velociraptors are carnivores by definition and no amount of talking would dissuade them otherwise. Stakeholders, with the exception of some anti-globalisation protestors, are not implicitly anti-business. Perhaps it would have been better (albeit less glamorous) for Peters to choose an omnivore for his analogy.

By engaging with civil society and reporting on their responsibility performance leaders are building trust through enhanced transparency. The laggards however are fighting back, to use the most obvious example, despite universal condemnation of its stance on climate change, it is often suggested that Exxon Mobil Corp. effectively contributed to the Bush administration's rejection of the Kyoto treaty. It has even allegedly funded incredulous scientists and trade associations (like the Global Climate Coalition) to lobby on its behalf. *The Economist* recently ran an article about Lee Raymond, the CEO of Exxon Mobil Corp. entitled 'The unrepentant oilman'. In the article Mr Raymond dismisses renewable energy as a 'Complete waste of money' (*The Economist*, 2003). Greenpeace and Friends of the Earth, through their spin-off 'Stop-Esso,'[28] have mounted daily protests against the corporate policies of Exxon, successfully closing large numbers of Exxon petrol stations and defacing the Esso brand. As yet this policy of confrontation, so successful when used against Shell and BP, has had little visible effect. Lee Raymond's Exxon Mobil Corp. remains one of the most profitable companies on earth. Clearly societal action, in its current form, has its limits.

2.5.3.2 Socially responsible investment (SRI)

The competitive advantage to be gained from behaving in a responsible manner is not however entirely intangible. Over the last 20 years a growing number of individuals and institutional investors have sought to ensure that their money was invested in companies that meet specific criteria for ethical and environmental behaviour. This trend was instigated in the US, where religious groups (primarily the Quakers) wanted to ensure that their money was not invested in the arms industry, tobacco, alcohol, gambling or South Africa (during Apartheid). As social and environmental issues have come to prominence, more and more people have chosen to adopt this discriminatory method of investing. The exact amount of money that is invested in a socially and environmentally responsible manner globally is difficult to gauge. However, according to the Social Investment Forum 'nearly one out of eight dollars under professional management in the US today is involved in socially responsible investing (Social Investment Forum, 2001)'. This equates to nearly '12 percent of the total US$19.9 trillion in investment assets under professional management in the US (Ibid)'. Sparkes estimates that in the United Kingdom in 2001 assets of £225bn were associated with SRI – this equates to roughly £4,000 for every person in Britain (Sparkes, 2002). Although this is a relatively small portion of total investments, and probably smaller still when considered on a global scale, it is not insignificant and should not be ignored by companies.

According to the United Kingdom Social Investment Forum there are two primary investment strategies that can be used by SRI investors, either separately or in combination (UK Social Investment Forum, 2003):

1. **Screening** refers to the practice of including or excluding stocks and shares from investment portfolios based upon ethical, environmental or social criteria. Funds can operate a *negative screening* strategy, in other words, they will simply not invest in unacceptable companies. Alternatively, a *positively screened* index will only comprise those companies who can demonstrate superior ethical, environmental or social performance.
2. **Shareholder Advocacy or engagement** refers to the process by which investors seek to improve corporate policy/performance through exercising their ownership rights. Investors will seek to engage corporate leadership and where not possible, file proxy resolutions forcing behavioural changes.

The effectiveness of the second strategy, 'shareholder advocacy', as a change catalyst has recently been tested and confirmed by the California Public Employees Retirement System (CALpers), the group that manages California's State pension fund (the largest American public pension scheme). In early April 2003 the management of CALpers sent GlaxoSmithKline (GSK), the UK-based pharmaceutical giant, a letter expressing its deep concern at the high prices charged for its AIDS drugs in the developing world. At the time CALpers held nearly US$260 million in GSK stock. In the letter CALpers stated that they felt that GSK was exposing itself to an unacceptable level of reputational risk (heavily impacting the value of their investment) by maintaining its current policy. Although GSK's immediate response was simply a re-emphasis of their policy by the end of the month the price of 'Combivir', the company's popular AIDS therapy, was reduced by 47 per cent. GSK claimed that the reduction was long planned, but obviously speculation was rife.

As a result of the recent growth in SRI funds, banks themselves appear to be more engaged in the corporate sustainability field than their peers in other sectors. This is qualified by the *UNEP Statement by Financial Institutions on the Environment and Sustainable Development*. Globally, the statement represents the single largest sectoral initiative in the field of corporate sustainability. Since 1992 over 190 financial institutions have committed to the 'integration of environmental considerations into all aspects of their operations (United Nations Environment Programme, 1997)'.

2.5.4 Combined impact of drivers

It has been shown that appropriate laws can act as a stimulus for innovation: they can also force laggards into action. The influence of morality as a driver should not be underestimated, but equally, as the Enron case shows us, it is not to be relied upon. The 'could' argument is likely to offer corporations the maximum return on investment. However, this benefit does not come without exposure to considerable risk. To extract advantage business needs come to terms with its role as an inclusive part of society. If it contributes towards common societal goals then it will be allowed to derive benefit (in terms of profit) from it.

In terms of achieving the long term goal of Sustainable Development, it would seem that only a combination of the three approaches will deliver the paradigm change required.

2.6 Demonstrating performance

We have discovered that companies have developed a number of innovative ways to tackle the issues that Sustainable Development poses; logically, the next question asks how and why companies demonstrate their performance. Obviously if the objective is responsibility for responsibilities' sake then demonstration is not overtly important. However, as in the majority of cases, if the company concerned wants to avoid risk and perhaps extract competitive advantage then this becomes of enormous importance. If stakeholders are unaware of the performance of business then there is a chance that they will erroneously exercise their influence. As Brent Spar showed us, even if the company concerned is acting justly, through poor communication stakeholders can be easily misled into backing the wrong horse.

Companies have responded to the need to communicate using the following strategies (individually or in combination):

- reporting
- marketing and Public Relations
- adherence to voluntary international standards

2.6.1 Reporting

Over the past 10 or 15 years the practice of reporting on environmental and social performance has developed rapidly. France, Denmark, Sweden, Holland, Australia and now the UK are either planning to or already require mandatory reporting of certain aspects of sustainability performance, but they remain the exception – the majority of reporting companies do so voluntarily. Initially companies started to reveal just environmental performance data – in the USA for example, this was an extended response to the Toxic Release Inventory (TRI, 1986) legislation. Over the next few years environmental reporting became more sophisticated and the companies involved were seeking some form of standardisation. In 1993, SustainAbility, the International Institute for Sustainable Development and Deloitte Touche produced a landmark report summarising interviews with the leaders of the environmental reporting fraternity (SustainAbility Ltd, UNEP, IISD, and Deloitte Touche, 1993). The report, a variant of which is now produced annually, identified a series of trends and developments in the area. SustainAbility used the report to encourage firms to begin to report along the TBL, that is, to report holistically on environmental, social and financial performance. A variety of reports produced by United Nations Environment Programme (UNEP) and a range of consultancies tracked the subsequent rise of corporate interest (KPMG and UvA, 2002; KPMG and WIMM, 1999; SustainAbility Ltd and UNEP, 1996, 1997, 1998, 2000; SustainAbility Ltd *et al.*, 1993). To exemplify this, in 1996 UNEP and SustainAbility estimated that there were approximately 300–400 environmental reports published annually, in 1999 KPMG were able to identify over 1100. Latest estimates suggest that this figure is now of the order of 2000.

Following this trend, there have been calls for standardisation of corporate sustainability reporting methodology. The Global Reporting Initiative (GRI) is the most high profile and successful project to emerge from this debate. The GRI is a voluntary 'multi-stakeholder process and independent institution whose mission is to develop and disseminate globally applicable Sustainability Reporting Guidelines' (Global Reporting Initiative, 2003). The guidelines are able to work in conjunction with UN Secretary-General Kofi Annan's Global Compact and have been adopted by over 600 businesses worldwide, including many prominent Global Fortune 500 companies. In the United Kingdom the government advocates the practice of sustainability reporting, having produced its own guidelines for environmental reporting (DEFRA, 2001) Prior to their publication, in a keynote address to the Confederation of British Industry (CBI), Prime Minister Tony Blair told business leaders: 'I would also like to see more reporting on environmental and social performance. I am issuing a challenge, today, to all of the top 350 companies to be publishing annual environment reports by the end of 2001' (Ibid). In reality only 79 companies rose to the challenge, but many of those companies are large and influential. The trend can be expected to flow down the supply chain in the near future. It now looks likely that reporting in a formal way on environmental, social and economic performance will become necessary for large businesses in the next 5–10 years. This will be achieved either through stakeholder pressure or governmental legislation.

Over the last five years governments in the Netherlands, in Sweden, France, Norway and Denmark have all enacted legislation covering aspects of the reporting of non-financial information. In July 2003 the UK government announced that it planned to require certain companies to produce Operating and Financial Reviews (OFRs) as a supplement in their annual financial reviews. This legislation has since come into force and now requires large UK quoted companies to make a legally binding statement, setting out the drivers of their company's performance both in the past and in the future. The exact nature of these drivers is left to the discretion of individual directors, but seems likely in the majority of cases to include a number of environmental and social issues. At the time of writing it is not clear how companies will react to this legislation, but I suspect that it will result in preparers consulting armies of lawyers and adopting an unnecessarily risk averse approach.

2.6.2 Marketing and PR

Companies have always sought to utilise marketing muscle to extract maximum competitive advantage from a given situation. The concept of sustainability is no exception to the rule.

There are many examples of good practice, where advertising claims are supported by action and verified by an external partner. However some unscrupulous businesses have observed the public's affinity with so called 'soft issues' and have designed 'phoney' marketing campaigns to exploit the issues and generate advantage without subsance.

Where efforts are unsubstantiated; Stakeholders often dismiss the presented image as 'greenwash' ('socially and environmentally destructive corporations attempting to preserve and expand their markets by posing as friends of the environment and leaders in the struggle to eradicate poverty'), 'bluewash' ('the humanitarian-themed variant of greenwash – companies touting their commitment to humanitarian causes like poverty eradication, disaster relief, human rights and sustainable development') or 'sweatwash' ('companies notorious for use of sweatshop labour trying to divert attention from their factories' practices'). As *CorpWatch* notes, 'You've seen the ads. Lush green forests. Stunning birds of prey in flight. Humpback whales breaching. Pristine streams glimmering in the sunlight. All photographed beautifully and reproduced at great expense. And all brought to you by major oil, chemical, nuclear and biotechnology companies. In fact, it's often the world's most polluting corporations that have developed the most sophisticated techniques to communicate their message' (CorpWatch.com, 2003). Bad behaviour by the minority has resulted in a climate of mistrust and suspicion that all businesses have to operate within.

Nike, the US-based sportswear company, is one of the largest companies to have been accused of this 'offence'. Between the late 1990s and 2003 they fought a high-profile court case in California over allegedly false responsibility performance claims made in publicly released documentation (*Kasky* v. *Nike*). Marc Kasky sued Nike for false advertising over a publicity campaign it used to defend itself against accusations that its footwear was made using child labour in Asian sweatshops.

The case centred on the difference between 'political speech' and 'commercial speech'; political speech being entitled to special protection in the Constitution of the US under the First Amendment (i.e. the protection of free speech). Commercial speech on the other hand is not protected to the same extent, and companies have an obligation to be truthful in their advertising claims.

After a great deal of controversial debate the court ruled that Nike's publicly released documentation should be considered as 'commercial speech' as it could potentially affect consumers' opinions about the company as a responsible business, and thereby affect their purchasing decisions. Justice Joyce L. Kennard stated that, 'Our holding, based on decisions of the United States Supreme Court, in no way prohibits any business enterprise from speaking out on issues of public importance or from vigorously defending its own labour practices. It means only that when a business enterprise, to promote and defend its sales and profits, makes factual representations about its own products or its own operations, it must speak truthfully.'

At this stage Nike made the decision to settle out of court with Marc Kasky. The US$1.5 million that they were forced to donate to the US Fair Labor Association as settlement would likely fade into insignificance when compared with the damage to their 'multi-billion' dollar brand had they continued to fight.

From the legal perspective it seems that there are only two solutions to the *Kasky* v. *Nike* debacle: one, to restrict free speech amongst society, or two, to give businesses a licence to mislead stakeholders. There is however an alternative, to make sustainability reporting subject to similar rules that govern financial reporting. Stakeholders would be free to challenge statements and data presented as fact in a clear, transparent and predefined manner. As it stands, Nike's decision to settle out of court means that the decision of the court remains intact, and the flood gates have been left open for other individuals to challenge commercial speech.

From the corporate perspective closing more doors and decreasing transparency is the most obvious response to this kind of ruling; it is not, however, the most sensible and sustainable option. In order to avoid accusations of this nature, multinationals (in terms of legality, most operate at some level in California) will need to be, first, more accurate and, second, overtly transparent, thereby instilling a level of trust that competitors would be deeply envious of.

Competitors would be envious because the public does not trust big business *per se*, in fact the public does not even trust elected officials. Every year for the past two decades Robert Worcester, Chairman of Market & Opinion Research International (MORI), has produced what he calls a 'Veracity Index': worryingly his research shows that on average the British public trusts trade union officials and television presenters far more than business leaders or politicians (see, www.mori.com for more information). Over two decades now, MORI's data shows that business leaders and politicians have been engaged in a head-to-head 'race to the bottom'. Ever since the onset of globalisation, marketing and branding experts have been frantically looking for ways to buck this trend, the ultimate goal being securing sustainable loyalty – perhaps they were looking in the wrong direction.

It would seem that trust could represent the competitive advantage of responsibility. Business needs look no further – trust is the business case for responsibility. It is simple psychology: if people trust a business, they will do business with it; they will 'elect' it as their partner of choice. Just look at the difference in initial public reaction between the transformations of Shell and BP. Triggered by several high profile PR disasters Shell chose to embark upon a transparent campaign, engaging stakeholders and improving responsibility performance. Under the leadership of Lord Browne, BP certainly improved their responsibility performance, but arguably did not immediately enhance transparency to the same extent. To symbolise this move they changed their branding – a move that cynics could, and did, easily pull apart (for example a number of sites on the internet have created spoof adverts suggesting that BP stands for Big Porkies).[29] A company that had recently acquired several large US companies could hardly trade in a notoriously nationalistic market with the original brand: *British Petroleum*. The new brand (a green and yellow star and the monogram 'BP', usually accompanied by the catchphrase '*beyond petroleum*') is, without a doubt, inspired; however, without the prerequisite transparency, and stakeholders were initially wary of it (see Murphy, 2002). This case proves that companies can alter their performance, but still stumble by creating the wrong image at the wrong time. Despite the above, BP's new brand is probably a success; however, it could have been a sensation. To return to Shell, despite their positive start, by massively overstating their oil reserves in 2003 they managed to very quickly erode the trust that they had spent the last few years building. Behind the scenes they had gone a long way towards changing the corporate culture, but 'closed doors' boardroom decisions made this action largely irrelevant. Now they are starting from the bottom again, working their way up, building broken bridges.

Clearly corporate marketing and PR initiatives represent highly dangerous ground for companies. As a result of this they are increasingly turning towards other mediums of communication, at least in the first instance. Despite some companies learning from the mistakes of others, we are likely to see many more examples of 'greenwash' in the near future before companies look for alternatives *en mass*.

2.6.3 Adherence to voluntary international standards and guidelines

By signing up to a selection of the myriad of local, national and international standards and guidelines related to sustainability businesses are (whilst achieving other objectives) demonstrating to their stakeholders that they are both engaged and serious about the subject matter. Examples of some of the more prominent programmes include:

- UN Global Compact,
- OECD Guidelines,
- Q-Res Guidelines,
- CERES Principles,
- Global Reporting Initiative,
- AA 1000,
- Global Sullivan Principles,
- Caux Round Table Principles,
- Ethical Trading Initiative,
- ICC Business Charter for Sustainable Development.

On the whole, signing up to voluntary initiatives suggests a commitment over and above simple legislative compliance. On the cynical side, it is worth pointing out that many of these standards and guidelines have no method for ensuring compliance – or removing signatories in the face of malpractice. In these cases signing up could be considered a win-win situation. A good example of this is the United Nations Global Compact. Initiated by Secretary General Kofi Annan in 1999, it comprises a list of nine commitments towards best practice in the field of corporate responsibility. Unfortunately, the Compact Secretariat has no power to investigate its signatories' practices, or to remove laggards. Meanwhile the association with the United Nations *whiter than white* image is likely to do the company concerned no end of good in terms of increased brand value.

2.7 Summary

At the close of this chapter it is useful to reflect on its title – 'Corporate Conscientiousness'. It seems clear that this phenomenon, while seemingly apparent, is not entirely natural or new. A historical perspective demonstrates that the relatively recent trend of globalisation has changed the way that societies view corporate behaviour. Issues like global environmental protection and the development of global societal capital that have been long forgotten are coming to the fore. Society at large has considered the issues and introduced the concept of 'Sustainable Development' as a potential way for individuals, organisations and governments alike to address the challenge.

Business is struggling to meet this challenge. The leading (but not dominant) immediate corporate response strategy – 'the apparent development of a conscience' – is varied, inconsistent, localised, and in many cases restricted to very large multinational corporations. The seemingly dominant corporate response strategy is to continue 'business as usual'. But perhaps we should not 'judge a book by its cover', perhaps companies are planning for change. The survey-based research outlined in Chapters 4 and 5 engages corporate leadership on one aspect/foundation of the business case – corporate reputation – and seeks to investigate planned future MNC response strategy. By ascertaining the position of environmental and social credibility within this strategy we can predict whether the development of a corporate conscientiousness (as outlined in this chapter) is here to stay or whether it is simply the latest in a long line of short-lived corporate trends.

3
Profiling Corporate Imagery: Seven Competitive Elements

3.1 Introduction

Advice from the bestseller book *The 48 Laws of Power* suggests that 'Reputation is the cornerstone of power. Through reputation alone you can intimidate and win; once it slips, however, you are vulnerable, and will be attacked on all sides. Make your reputation unassailable. Always be alert to potential attacks and thwart them before they happen' (Greene and Elffers, 1998).

While clearly this perspective is just a little on the Machiavellian side its main point stands. Corporate reputation is more than just important, it can be all consuming. This is particularly the case when like Nike or Coca-Cola your imagery is your only 'real' value. But, contrary to popular belief, it is certainly not restricted to companies with business models of that nature. Remember that every business has customers, they might not be individuals, but they are still highly likely to be human! And all humans without exception are subject to the influencing power of imagery.

This chapter offers a new and dissimilar look at the origins and future of corporate and organisational reputation. From the outset it is written with an awareness of the rising importance of Corporate Sustainability/Responsibility. After clarifying/defining the key terms, I move on to examine the process of image formation within the corporate sphere. I then look at how different organisations have attempted to quantify reputation, what methodologies they have used, and how useful the results are. The current body of knowledge has been rationalised forming seven competitive elements of reputation. I will argue that rather than attempting to manage 'reputation' *per se*, rather than counting and ranking things that arguably cannot be counted, companies should strive to manage the sources of reputation. Manage, perform and communicate effectively in these areas and a company can more or less influence the perception that key stakeholders have of them.

3.2 Reputation and its alternate guises

All products, services and organisations engender images. These images are created and managed by both the organisation itself and its stakeholders. Organisations have traditionally exclusively managed this image using a variety of time-honoured propaganda techniques. Things have changed: the Internet, as an example of one of today's liberated and most influential propaganda machines, is not exclusively under the influence of corporations. Stakeholders have also become more powerful, dispersing divergent and increasingly penetrative forms of propaganda. As these new medias force organisations to increase their transparency, the corporate character is left exposed and under threat. This predicament is not solely restricted to corporations, Peter van Ham – writing in the journal *Foreign affairs* – states that, 'Globalisation and the media revolution have made each state more aware of itself, its image, its reputation, and its attitude.' Further stating that this implies 'a shift in political paradigms, a move from the modern world of geopolitics and power to the post-modern world of images and influence' (Van Ham, 2001).

Imagery is a term not often used in the corporate arena, here it is used as a 'catch-all' idiom, referring to all of the induced perceptions or appearances surrounding a 'subject' (in this case the subject is a company but the concept applies equally to individuals). The significance of corporate imagery is based on the importance of appearances in defining one company from its competitors. Barney concurs suggesting that reputation is an important resource that enterprises can use to extract competitive advantage (Barney, 2002). Ultimately, if there is nothing which defines one company from another then there is no reason for consumers to select one product or service over and above another.

Any discussion of corporate imagery will inevitably draw on a diverse base of cross-disciplinary terminology, for example, 'corporate image', 'corporate identity', 'corporate reputation' and perhaps 'corporate character'. These terms are sometimes used interchangeably in reference to the same concept (Grunig, 1993; Wartick, 2002). Key opinion-formers have tended to adopt certain individual terms as their own personal concepts and, as a result, almost all subsequent peer-reviewed literature is 'required' to subscribe to, and to build upon, their interpretation, in many cases overlooking the original meaning of the word. With few

Table 3.1 Abridged *Oxford Dictionary* terminology *(Sykes, 1982)*

Character	Distinctive mark, Collective peculiarities, Person's or race's idiosyncrasy, Reputation.
Identity	Individuality, personality, condition of being a specified person.
Image	Artificial imitation of the external form of an object. Character of a thing or person as perceived by the public. Optical appearance.
	The word image is derived from the Latin *imitari* meaning: imitation.
Reputation	What is generally said or believed about a person's or thing's character. The word reputation is derived from the Latin *reputatio-onis* meaning: 1. calculation 2. thought, estimate, consideration

exceptions, this ongoing process has led to an overt complication of an otherwise simple concept.

Before going any further I will define what I understand each of the terms to mean – in their most basic form (Table 3.1 outlines the basic dictionary definitions of each word). Although these definitions do not relate specifically to their contextual business setting, they do provide us with a commonly accepted base for making further interpretation, giving a broad understanding of their meaning.

In reading these definitions obvious parallels can quickly be drawn between *character* and *identity* and between *image* and *reputation*. *Character* and *identity* appear to be linked by a relative lack of external influence. *Image* and *reputation* are interpretations, controlled by public perceptions and general beliefs.

At a glance it would seem that character and identity are analogous, however they can be separated at two levels. First, identity refers to the conditions that determine individuality. Character however implies behavioural-based idiosyncrasies, peculiar to an individual. It represents the difference between physical fact and behavioural reality. The way a person, object or organisation acts can be different from the way a person, object or organisation looks.

This analysis of 'character' is supported by Stephen Covey, who suggests that 'character, basically is a composite of our habits. Sow a thought, reap an action; sow an action, reap a habit; sow a habit, reap a character; sow a character, reap a destiny' (Covey, 1989). Covey defines a habit as the 'intersection of knowledge, skill and desire' (Ibid). That is, knowing what to do, how to do it, and finally having the aspiration to do it. Having capabilities in these key areas can provide individuals – and companies (groups of individuals) – with enhanced effectiveness, leading to character-building with reputational implications.

Returning to the dictionary definitions, *image* and *reputation* are also closely linked. Both refer to what appears to be there, rather than what is actually there. The difference being that images are determined by the individual; reputation refers to holistic, generally held beliefs. Therefore, using dictionary definitions alone, we can conclude that reputations are constructed from multiple dynamic images; images that are constructed from identity and more importantly character.

Simple dictionary definitions also reveal an interesting perspective on the development of these concepts over time. Because *character* and *identity* are determined primarily by the subject themselves (individual or organisation) they are unlikely to change dramatically in a short period of time (with the obvious exception of internal re-branding/re-naming programmes); in fact it would appear that they are both relatively stable. In contrast, *image* and *reputation* are both grounded in the perception and interpretation of multiple actors; this is something that is inherently dynamic and therefore highly unlikely to remain constant for long periods of time. Reputation is in a constant state of flux.

3.3 The process of image formation

At start up, a firm has little in the way of a reputation, it has not yet built up brand value and it will not have been the subject of mature images. It will, however, have an identity, that is, it will have peculiarities that collectively form its character. Albert and Whetten define organisational identity[30] as being 'that which is central, enduring, and distinctive about an organization's culture' (Albert and Whetten, 1985). In other words, identity is a self-constructed concept founded upon corporate values and culture, at least at the beginning. Following on from this perspective, Gioia suggests that, 'at best, a *bona fide* identity appears to "exist" only in the first stages of an organization's history, but it soon becomes subject to the significant influence of image' (Gioia, 2000). Scott and Lane build on Albert and Whetten's work, suggesting that organisational identity can be described as 'the set of beliefs shared between top managers and stakeholders about the central, enduring, and distinctive characteristics of an organisation' (Albert and whetten, 1985;

Scott and Lane, 2000). I disagree with the idea that stakeholders have a great influence over identity, they are more often than not presented with an identity by the company and then they subsequently interact generating images and character.

As we have already discovered, from shortly after its formation to its demise a company is surrounded by many images, the sum of which can be referred to as *reputation* (a 'macro' image). I accept Fombrun and Shanley's stakeholder-based definition of *reputation* that reputations represent publics' cumulative judgments of firms over time (Fombrun and Shanley, 1990). Following this, *character* and *image,* as perceived and actual representations, have an important role to play. As stated earlier, at start-up, stakeholders have yet to form an *image* that is dramatically different from the presented *identity*. As time passes and the newly formed organisation interacts with its stakeholders, the untainted *image* or *identity* passes through a reality check, that is, stakeholders question whether the corporate *identity* in fact reflects reality. It is at this stage that mutations can occur to the initial *identity*, subsequently affecting insiders' perception of their own *identity* (Gioia, 2000). *Image* can help to bolster *identity*, alternatively it can damage it, and vice versa. But where does *character* fit into this? *Character* is often something that is acquired over time; older people are often referred to as being 'quite a *character*', the same is true of organisations. *Character* is not however linked to age, it is linked to 'collective peculiarities', and these can be acquired at any stage during the life of an individual or organisation. I argue that *identity* is superseded in importance by *character* in the early stages of an organisation's history. Gioia (Ibid) suggests that 'organizational *identity* forms the basis for the development and projection of images, which are then received by outsiders, given their own interpretations and fed back into the organization in modified form'. Following my argument, this modified form represents the emergent corporate *character*. Although *character* does not necessarily have a strong time element, the same is not true of *reputation* which appears to be aggregated over a period of years and decades. Petrick *et al*. concur suggesting that reputations are 'usually the product of years of demonstrated superior competence' (Petrick *et al*., 1999), and 'trustworthy behaviour' (Hosmer, 1995). Consequentially, they are a fragile resource that take time to build, cannot be bought, and can easily be damaged. Summarising, corporate character is a dynamic concept, continually affected by stakeholder images both at a 'micro' (individual images) and 'macro' (reputational) level. Problems occur when the two come out of alignment and perceived images deviate from character-based behaviour (see the *Shell Brent Spar* case in Section 3.4).

3.3.1 The stability of corporate identities

Despite the importance of corporate character, corporate identity remains of fundamental importance. It is the starting point for companies wishing to alter the imagery surrounding them. To take an example, Philip Morris Companies Inc. (a renowned American manufacturer of cigarettes and other consumer goods) recently decided to change its identity. They claimed that

> the introduction of Altria [their new name] reflects important evolutions in [their] development. The name Philip Morris is truly a tobacco name – a name associated with a remarkable history as a leader in that industry both in the United States and around the world. But [they] also have come to own a number of companies that are not tobacco-based, companies such as *General Foods, Kraft, Jacobs Suchard* and *Nabisco*. By changing [their] name, *Altria Group* will clarify its identity as what it is: a parent company to both tobacco and food companies that manage some of the world's most successful brands (Altria Group, 2003).

This official interpretation is hotly contested[31] but nevertheless it represents a genuine attempt to alter perceptions through identity modification. Just the fact that they have a web page detailing their corporate identity signifies the relative stability of the concept. Visitors to Altria's website can even take part in the 'Altria identity challenge' – to ensure that they have correctly understood the new identity. Altria Group is clearly hoping that this new identity will permanently alter their character, resulting in an improved imagery and consequentially an improved reputation.[32]

Despite this example, dramatically adjusting corporate identity is not a common phenomenon. Many companies (particularly those with a strong brand value) are careful not to tamper with their original identity, straying from a successful formula. Consider for example, Coca-Cola, Johnson & Johnson, Hewlet Packard, McDonalds and even Cambridge University as cases in point. In these and other cases it is the enduring nature of identity that contributes towards sustainable competitive advantage.

3.3.2 Stakeholder perspectives

Stakeholders, as defined by Freeman,[33] are instrumental in the formation of corporate imagery. Consumers are one of a company's most important stakeholders, if a company cannot sell its product or service it will not last for very long. According to Herbig and Milewicz, 'consumers use reputation as a means of inferring quality of the product' (Herbig and Milewicz, 1997). As most successful companies know, quality is defined as 'conformance to requirements' (Crosby, 1979b). It is equally well known that these requirements are set by the customer, 'who is always right'.[34] Simplistically speaking if a company is able to meet customer demands it will benefit from an enhanced reputation. However, the customer–producer relationship is no longer simple and to fully capitalise on their intangible assets today's company must do far more than just meet customer demands. The twenty-first century company must try to meet, or be seen to be constructively engaging with all of its stakeholders.

Again, following Freeman's definition (Freeman, 1984) clearly firms have more than one stakeholder, therefore it is reasonable to suggest that firms too are pictured by more than one image. Fill and Diminopolu have studied the formation of corporate images and conclude that 'Images are inherently multidimensional and it is unlikely that all stakeholders will share the same image at any one point in time' (Fill and Diminopolu, 1999). Following on from this, *image*, like beauty, is in the eye of the beholder. Consequentially, the values assigned to reputational attributes will express significant variance depending on both the observer/stakeholder and the filter through which they receive their information.

As I have already acknowledged, organisations do have an inclusive *image* at a 'macro' level, known commonly as *reputation* (Fombrun, 1996). Stakeholders however are not usually able to take an objective/holistic view of *reputation* before choosing to buy/use/invest, and so on. The individual's tainted perception of corporate *image* is clearly the defining factor. This is emphasised in Figure 3.1 where individual by perceived images are considered independently. The macro or theoretical *reputation* clearly refers to the sum of multiple individual images.

Figure 3.2 takes this concept one step further. By specifically expanding on the arrows in Figure 10 the process of image formation is detailed. I argue that all images are received through a series of filters. In what Pratkanis et al termed 'The Age of Propaganda' (Pratkanis & Aronson, 1991), the differing strength of these filters affects reputations.

As can be seen in Figure 3.2 an organisation's initial (or subsequentially altered) *identity* or *self* passes first through an external filter; this filter is constructed of other stakeholders' perceived images. Some of these images will be more powerful (and therefore more persuasive) than others. Individuals will rarely see beyond the first filter – almost as soon as the organisation is launched (or re-launched) its *identity* is dynamically affected by its stakeholders. Internal and external images of the organisation are affected by perceptions, and the resulting behavioural changes form the basis of *character*. The strength of the second external

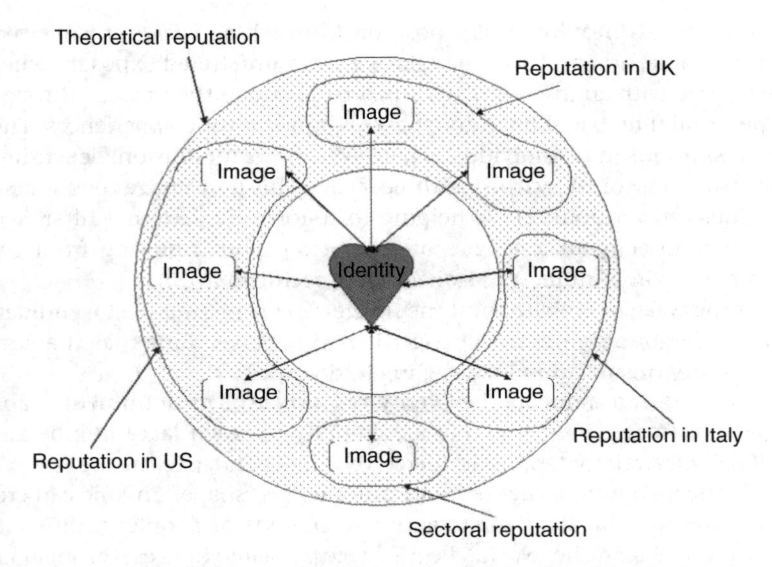

Figure 3.1 A simplified example of the relationship between identity, image and reputation.

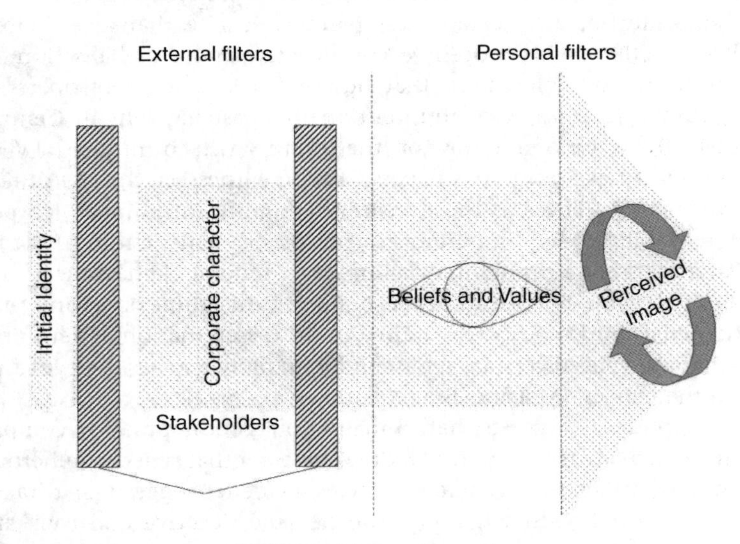

Figure 3.2 The process of individual image formation.

filter depends heavily on the position from which *character* is viewed. For example, an employee may have greater unfettered exposure when compared with an investor. This 'distorted' *image* is then passed through a personal filter based on individual beliefs, values and experiences. This process results in an individually perceived *image* (or illusion, depending on your viewpoint), warped at three levels. This new image then joins a 'vicious' or 'virtuous' circle helping to re-form the external filter. The external filter is an analogue of reputation, both resulting from the reconciliation of numerous stakeholder specific images.

In the wake of globalisation the image filtering power of stakeholders has undergone significant change, it is this power shift that the contemporary organisation is struggling to delineate.

The media are arguably the twenty-first century's most influential and powerful image filter; they have the ability to reach large numbers of people with relative ease and 'perceived' independence. In the last ten years the media circus has dramatically changed shape. Anyone can create a website and have direct access to billions of people in different countries across the world. People receive daily images through an increasingly diverse number of information sources, for example, newspaper, Internet, mail, telephone, posters, TV, radio, flyers and personal communication. In effect, over the last twenty years this has resulted in a dramatic increase in the number of connections/interactions between stakeholders. In this 'smaller world' our 'Network Society' (see Castells, 1996) operates at a faster and less predictable rate than ever before (Willmott, 2001). This process, a constituent part of globalisation, is removing the veil of secrecy that business has historically operated under (albeit in most cases unintentional). What happens in Central Africa in the afternoon is now on the Internet within minutes, TV in hours and in next morning's papers. We are witnessing the rise of *real time reactionism*. This has the potential to significantly impact corporate profitability. More importantly what happens in Central Africa in the afternoon has the potential to impact stakeholder behaviour in the evening. McLane, Bratic and Bersin highlight this point observing that 'With media continuously expanding for the dissemination of news and information, alleged corporate misconduct rapidly reaches the eyes and ears of the masses' (McLane, Bratic, and Bersin, 1999).

This hypothesis suggests that to maintain a good reputation companies must actively try to build a flexible character that reflects numerous fast moving stakeholder generated images. Evidence suggests that stakeholders respect honesty. If images do become negative and they are grounded in reasonable fact, it makes sense for the company concerned to admit that things went wrong. Together with an action plan designed to prevent future occurrences, this process defies claims of corporate arrogance, and retains valuable reputation. The examples below show that the acknowledgement of mistakes and high-profile adoption of a new transparent, responsive character can prevent the erosion of reputational capital:

- *Johnson & Johnson* In 1982, seven people suddenly died after having innocently taken *Tylenol* 'pain-killer' capsules. After investigation, the FBI discovered that the capsules had been tampered with and deliberately laced with cyanide. Prior to this event, *Tylenol* had command of 37 per cent of the market, capturing US $400 million in annual sales. Despite the fact that Johnson & Johnson were found not guilty of any misconduct, their stock price fell by 29 per cent and their market share dropped to 6 per cent. Johnson & Johnson embarked on the largest product recall ever undertaken, they shut down production and distribution and tested over 8 million bottles. The company followed a policy of transparency; they sponsored full-page newspaper advertisements, wrote stories for the media and opened a major call centre. By working with the FBI and taking actions that did not make short-term financial sense Johnson & Johnson ensured the long-term survival of the brand and salvaged their own reputation. (For further information see Dowdell, Govindaraj and Jain, 1992.)

This example can be contrasted with the recent conduct of Firestone Inc., confirming that many companies have not yet discovered how to protect their reputation when confronted by 'disaster':

- *Firestone Inc./Ford Motor Company* In 2000, Firestone was forced to recall a number of its tyres after it was alleged that on some models the tread had a tendency to separate from the rim. A number of contemporary investigations have connected the tyres with 203 deaths and at least 250 injuries. Firestone's biggest customer The Ford Motor Company fitted Firestone tyres as standard on many of its Sport Utility Vehicles (SUV). The problem therefore required a dual response. Firestone acted first, denying responsibility, citing both Ford and consumers for lack of maintenance and using the wrong tyre pressures. This rapid response, displaying almost unparalleled corporate arrogance was a big mistake; government investigations revealed that the fault lay firmly with the tyres and a recall was demanded. Firestone again blundered, they undertook the minimum possible action, recalling only 6.5 million tyres, not the entire product line. Both companies made mistakes during this episode shifting blame from one to another, mistakes that would later prove to be costly. Firestone's stock has been in a downward spiral ever since the event, and Ford cite the problem as a major contributory factor to poor sales and loss of market share in 2000/01. (For further information see: Knowledge@Wharton, 2003.)

Concluding this section, I argue that reputation can be described as a dynamically, self-adjusting blend of stakeholder generated, filtered images, viewed over an extended time period. It is clear that reputations should be viewed as being ephemeral, needing constant management attention to uphold them.

3.4 The value of positive imagery

As we discovered earlier, all organisations are surrounded by images. Following on from this and using my earlier definition of *character*, all organisations have *character*. This character can be leveraged to create value. Conversely it can be mismanaged, acting against a company's aspirations of growth. Overall, *character* has an intrinsic value, primarily because without it the organisation concerned would have difficulty marketing directly linked products or services. Companies would have difficulty managing/directing stakeholder generated images or building a resilient *reputation*.

Assuming that a company is directly linked to its branded products and/or services, poor reputation or negative imagery results in reduced consumer confidence, and a subsequent decline in brand value. Despite the well-acknowledged fact that brands represent an intangible asset, the consultancy Interbrand has pioneered a methodology designed to attempt to value them. This procedure makes it easier than ever to draw a tangible link between fluctuating image and the financial bottom line. Looking at the issue from a different angle, they endeavour to value the earnings stream that a brand creates 'The brand is an intangible asset that creates an identifiable economic earnings stream … . Brand value is defined as the net present value of the economic profit that the brand is expected to generate in the future' (Clifton and Maughan, 2000).

Considered together with the majority of past research, this suggests that reputation is a resource, albeit intangible, leading to competitive advantage (Barney, 2002; Deephouse, 2000; Fombrun, 1996; Hall, 1992);

the material advantage being primarily in the form of increased brand value. Looking at resources in greater depth requires a brief synthesis of the pre-eminent resource-based view (RBV) of the firm: a management theory focusing on competitive advantage derived from the resources and capabilities that a firm controls that are valuable, rare, imperfectly imitable and not substitutable (see Barney, 1991; Barney *et al.*, 2001; Caves, 1980; Deephouse, 2000; Hall, 1992; Werner-felt, 1984). These resources can be tangible or intangible, that is, some resources can be assigned a specific value (these are the easiest to manage, and consequentially to replicate) others cannot. To take a recent example, James Dyson, an inventor and eminent entrepreneur recently took it upon himself to redesign the vacuum cleaner. In doing so he was entering a marketplace saturated with established brand leaders like Hoover, Miele, Hitachi, Electrolux, Panasonic and others. He had to come up with something distinctive, something that would make his vacuum cleaner desirable in the face of cheaper, well-designed competition. He succeeded by patenting 'Dual Cyclone' technology, a revolutionary new way to perform an age-old task. The 'Brand Leaders' were taken by surprise and rapidly lost market share, James Dyson had entered the marketplace as a force to be reckoned with. Initially, companies like Hoover could only stand by and watch their market share decline. However, as time passed, they imitated him recreating the same, or similar technology removing the performance advantage that Dyson had created. They succeeded in recapturing some but by no means all of their market share. Why, surely if the two products looked and performed the same, the one offered by an established manufacturer should succeed? The answer can be found, but not calculated: the establishment could not recreate Dyson's intangibles, that is, his positive reputation for vision, leadership, innovation and quality products. *Dyson* vacuum cleaners are currently produced at the startling rate of 8000 per day and command half of the British market by value, annual worldwide sales now reach £3billion.[35] Dyson has now embarked on reinventing other household electrical appliances; competitors had better be on their guard. Dyson – with an established reputation – could pose an even greater threat.

Because of a preoccupation with managing tangible assets and unfamiliarity with how to competitively exploit the untapped value of a good reputation, many top management teams have failed to capitalise on the intangible resources of the firm (Hall, 1992). Court, Leiter and Loch highlight this failure and suggest that it can be a costly mistake; their analysis suggests that about half of the market value of the Fortune 250 is tied to intangible assets (Court, Leiter and Loch, 1999). Pertrick *et al.*, suggests that sustainable competitive advantage is the result of 'a distinctive capability differential due in large part to leveraging the intangible resources of leadership skills and reputational assets that are more difficult to substitute or imitate by competitors than tangible resources' (Petrick *et al.*, 1999). This is clearly the case in the Dyson example.

Globalisation has caused, among other things, an explosion of choice for the consumer (Willmott, 2001). This explosion of choice has changed the way that the twenty-first century consumer purchases products and services. According to Willmott, to cope with increased choice, the consumer adopts a series of different purchasing strategies, only one of which is tangible – price. The other three are choice on the basis of:

1. Brand
2. Independent advice
3. Values/ethical concerns

All of these choice-influencing factors are shaped at several levels by reputations, following the resource-based view of the firm; all three, if managed well, can provide competitive advantage. The consequences of mismanagement can be disastrous, both for the company concerned and for its valued brands. There are now a great number of examples (see list that follows) whereby communications savvy individuals and groups of united individuals have brought multi-billion dollar corporations to their knees over perceived environmental and social misdemeanours:

- *The Pharmaceutical Industry* (The Pharmaceutical Manufacturers' Association of South Africa) – the affordable AIDS drugs case: Over the last five to ten years the major global drugs companies have been investing heavily in the development of antiretroviral drugs, designed to alleviate the symptoms of HIV. These drugs, when taken in a complex cocktail, are effective at helping individuals with HIV to live relatively normal lives. They have however one drawback: because of the investment that drug companies have made in their development, they are expensive. This is not necessarily a problem in Western countries where national health services are able to foot the bill. However in the poorest parts of the world this represents a real obstacle. The problem is compounded by the fact that out of the estimated 36.1 million people worldwide who are infected with the HIV, more than 90 per cent of this total live in developing countries.

In 1997 the South African government decided that enough; was enough; they took advantage of the weak patent legislation in their country to pass a law allowing the country to import cheap alternatives to branded anti AIDS medicines. This was met by stiff opposition, both from the drug companies themselves, and from politicians. In the US, Al Gore, then running for President, announced that this decision would sour diplomatic relations between the two countries if he were to be elected. A coalition representing 39 leading drug companies brought a court case against the South African government. After a very vocal and well-publicised battle lasting three years the drug companies dropped their case, and after loosing an election Al Gore dropped his opposition. As a result, South Africa is now able to import non-branded drugs from India at a cost of c.US$350 a year, compared to c.US$1200 charged by the brand leaders. Combinations of available pharmaceuticals previously too expensive for nearly all of the infected people in South Africa could now enable many afflicted with HIV/AIDS to live relatively normal lives (for further information see BBC News, 2003). In an almost complete turnaround companies like US drug maker Merck & Co are now in the process of providing African countries with royalty-free licensing of their top-rated antiretroviral AIDS drugs.

Why did the drug companies drop this opportunity to realise a very profitable revenue stream? The answer is likely to lie in the negative publicity they were receiving in their home countries. Stakeholder pressure was causing undesired damage to the image of their sector. The cost–benefit equation did not add up. An example of this kind of 'home ground' brand damage could be found on the front page of *The Guardian* (a major and well respected British Broadsheet) on the 24 April 2003. The editors had doctored a fully branded image of a Pfizer medicine bottle, replacing the standard drug warning with 'Warning not to be taken by the world's poor'. Drug companies look set to suffer from further devaluations in their brand value before they take their stakeholders seriously.

Most recently drug companies have switched their attention to India, the world's most successful manufacturer and, more importantly, exporter of so-called generic drugs. Behind the scenes many of the more powerful drug companies have been using their trade associations to lobby the World Trade Organisation (WTO) to force the Indian government to implement WTO Trade Related Intellectual Property Rights (TRIPS) legislation. This inevitable legislation will outlaw the production of, among other things, generic drugs. Round one to the drug companies, but I suspect that this fight is not over.

- *Coca-Cola* – Greenhouse unfriendly refrigeration at the 'Green Olympics': Back in 2000 the Olympic committee pronounced the Sydney Olympic Games to be the 'Green Games', the most environmentally friendly ever. The Coca-Cola Company as a major sponsor was awarded exclusive rights to sell its soft drinks at the games. Much to Coca-Cola's satisfaction, everything seemed in order. However two months before the games were due to begin Greenpeace released its Dirty Sponsors report, suggesting that Coca-Cola were preparing to use large numbers of HFC emitting refrigerators to chill their drinks. Hydrofluorocarbons are a potent greenhouse gas, significantly contributing to climate change. Greenpeace instigated a major anti Coca-Cola campaign, using the internet as their primary medium (see, www.cokespotlight.org). One month later, the CEO of Coca-Cola was in face-to-face negotiations with a team from Greenpeace. The meeting concluded by Coca-Cola conceding that they would make significant changes to their global refrigeration policy. It was too late to have an impact at Sydney, but to the pleasure of Greenpeace, the new 'Greenfreeze' refrigerators were up and running throughout the Olympic games at Athens 2004. According to insiders, Greenpeace were shocked by the speed of Coca-Cola's response – they had prepared for a much longer battle.[36]

Coca-Cola may have capitulated, but in doing so they had saved their US$83 billion brand from significant damage, and awarded themselves a great deal of good publicity four years down the line in Athens.

- *Shell International* – the Brent Spar case: In 1994 Shell announced that it would be disposing of a disused oil storage platform (the Brent Spar). After some research, and stakeholder engagement, disposal at sea was considered to be the most appropriate option. The German arm of the international environmental NGO Greenpeace discovered this and conducted their own research, concluding that, instead, land disposal would have been a much better option. Greenpeace Germany then began a sustained high profile media campaign, heavily criticising Shell's decision. Throughout Europe, especially in Scandinavia and Germany a boycott of Shell's petrol was instigated. The intense pressure paid off and Shell was forced to mitigate further damage by aborting its plans. Once the platform had been safely returned to land, independent inspection revealed that Greenpeace's research was incorrect. The best environmental option was disposal at sea. This case suggests that doing the 'right thing' is not always the whole story (see Bate, 1995; Looney, 1996).

- *Shell International* – Human Rights in Nigeria: The following extract from *The Economist* entitled 'Helping, but not developing' briefly outlines the chain of events:

> Corporate images are as hard to clean up as oil spills, to judge by the experience of *Royal Dutch/Shell's* subsidiary in Nigeria. In 1995 the company's reputation suffered when the Nigerian government hanged Ken Saro-Wiwa, a political activist who had been demanding that oil companies pay millions of dollars to local villagers. *Shell* denied any responsibility for Saro-Wiwa's death. But it also set out to prove that it cared for the people who lived in its production areas (*The Economist*, 2001).
>
> Since then the company has poured more than US$150m into local development schemes. Independent analysis (Unicef, World Bank) reveals that 64 per cent were judged to be fully or partially successful.[37] Their reputation has arguably recovered some of its lost ground. However in order to return to previous levels their performance in all areas has to continue to equal the rhetoric.

Having a good reputation and highly valued brands is like having money in the bank. However if your bank is not secure you risk losing all of your hard earned money.

It may seem obvious but as Nolan points out in his 1975 *Harvard Business Review* article 'The essence of improving the business image rests not in trying to conjure up a good story when performance fails, but in sharpening corporate perceptions of emerging social and political trends and in adjusting performance so that there will, in fact be a good story to tell' (Nolan, 1975).

As we have just seen, a good environmental and social record could add to a favourable corporate reputation but taken alone it is not sufficient. This good record must be well managed and communicated, avoiding accusations of 'greenwashing'. Companies trying to improve their reputation should first ensure that their character is dynamic enough to reflect the constantly shifting demands of stakeholders before interfering with the filters. It is a delicate balance between risk and opportunity.

Stakeholder imagery created through experience can label a brand (or the entire organisation) with a poor reputation. Having a poor reputation is not however the end. During the 1980s and early 90s the western European Skoda owner was considered to be either mad or making an 'alternative' statement. At one stage it was fairly probable that once the

'Iron Curtain' fell the brand would be extinguished forever. However, Volkswagen, the reputationally valuable German automotive company bought the company and proceeded to re-launch *Skoda*. In 2000 Skoda sold one car every 52 seconds, enjoying total sales of over 450,000 units.[38] This compares to less than 350,000[39] *Rovers* – an established western brand – sold in the same period. This is an example of successful reputational capital transfer.

By effectively managing reputation, companies have the opportunity to build an unofficial contract of trust with their stakeholders. This contract can allow companies freedom to innovate, create brand extensions (e.g. *Virgin Atlantic, Virgin Megastores, Virgin Vie, Virgin Bank, Virgin Vodka*, and perhaps even *Virgin spaceships*) and grow within the brand's quality (what customers have come to expect) limits.

Reputational value has the potential to build or destroy brand value depending on how closely the mother company is linked to its brands. However, more frequently than not the situation works in reverse, that is, brand value builds and destroys reputations (again depending on the extent to which company and brand are related). A company may not appear to have extensive reputational capital to the vast majority of stakeholders; in this case its brand value is all that remains. A good example of this would be Philip Morris International and its parent company Altria Group, a company whose name does not enter the Interbrand top 100 world's most valuable brands, and arguably has little in the way of a positive reputation. Philip Morris does however produce the *Marlboro* brand of cigarettes, the world's tenth most valuable brand (Clifton and Mangham, 2000).

Summarising, a number of commentators have studied the different benefits of having a good or favourable reputation, following their research these benefits can be distilled into eight key areas:

1. The ability to charge a premium price for goods and services offered.
2. The crystallisation of a firm's status and subsequent creation of competitive barriers.
3. Enhanced access to capital markets.
4. Increased organisational attractiveness to prospective employees, coupled with greater retention rates.
5. Provision of a buffer zone of reputational capital to insulate against unintentional failures, that is, heightened consumer confidence.
6. Improved customer loyalty.
7. Increased attractiveness to investors.
8. Reduced marketing costs, for example, Marks and Spencer's did not feel the need to advertise during their 1970s, 80s and early 90s boom

period, their reputation said it all. This same model now applies to the American clothing accessories chain, Claire's Accessories (rapid global growth coupled with zero advertising, they rely purely on experience-based word of mouth) (Deephouse, 2000; Fombrun and Shanley, 1990; Kartalia, 2000; Turban and Greening, 1997).

3.4.1 Measuring the intangible, reputation quantification

New York University professor Charles Fombrun working in parallel with Harris Interactive (a research group) has endeavoured to delineate corporate reputation and develop a methodology to measure it. Using a series of focus groups across the US, the group questioned stakeholders about companies that they respected or not, as the case may be. When asked why they held strong opinions about individual companies stakeholders justified their position by citing one of twenty reputational attributes. The research group were then able to fit these components of reputation into six representative categories:

1. emotional appeal
2. products and services
3. financial performance
4. vision and leadership
5. workplace environment
6. social responsibility[40]

These components are measured by merging weighted opinions from stakeholder groups. The resulting 'Reputational Quotient'[41] (RQ) forms a 'benchmarkable' appraisal of reputation.

I argue that this model is useful in helping organisations to target areas for improvement; but as reputations are not mathematical in nature (or stable), weightings cannot be applied universally (e.g., global cultural differences mean that stakeholder behaviour in one market is no indication of behaviour in another). Reputations are built on peoples' dynamic mindsets and opinions, which are difficult, if not impracticable, to quantify. Equally, as Wartick points out, 'the most glaring omission is that only one stakeholder group (the general public) is the focus' (Wartick, 2002). The success of the RQ does not come as a surprise, it follows the traditional embedded management mindset that: in order to manage something, you have to be able to measure it (Enderle and Tavis, 1998). As a result of its undoubted marketability it also has support of a major broadsheet (the *Wall Street Journal*).

Clearly the best method of gauging corporate imagery involves getting out and talking to stakeholders; adding up their opinions (to form a measure of reputation) is however a far more complicated task. If the methodology behind the RQ has managed to accurately replicate the respective importance of stakeholders it would have stumbled upon one of the most powerful management tools ever seen.

Despite the obvious difficulties involved with valuing intangibles, a number of organisations periodically endeavour to rate the reputation of major companies, producing sought-after lists of the world's (and country specific) most admired companies. Because of the overtly commercial nature of these lists most of the data and methodology adopted is not available in the literature. It is interesting to note that in order to improve their reputations many commentators suggest that corporations should be more transparent, yet the lists that claim to rate reputations are far from transparent themselves.

Examples of these lists include:

- *Fortune*: World's most admired companies;
- *Far Eastern Economic Review*: Annual review;
- *Management Today*: Britain's most admired companies;
- *Financial Times*: Europe's most respected companies;
- *Asian Business*: Asia's most admired companies.

The methodology used for each of these surveys varies, but normally takes the form of a stakeholder specific appraisal. In the case of the most famous ranking, the *Fortune* list, that exclusive stakeholder is the business community. The underlying research only targets one group of stakeholders, business people, that is, the finance community, employees and others. *Fortune* arrive at each company's final reputational score by averaging scores that survey respondents provide on each of the following nine criteria:

1. innovativeness
2. quality of management
3. employee talent
4. use of corporate assets
5. long-term investment value
6. social responsibility
7. financial soundness
8. quality of products/services
9. global business acumen

Out of these nine, equally weighted key attributes of reputation, at least three explicitly relate to financial performance. Financial performance may be more important than the other indicators when viewed from the perspective of today's businessman/woman – but this is hardly an objective approach. To calculate reputation you would need to consult far more than one stakeholder. This ranking methodology therefore represents a one-sided picture of corporate reputation (Brown and Perry, 1994; Fryxell and Wang, 1994; Wartick, 2002). As an innovation from 2001 onwards, to be eligible, a company had to have annual revenues of US$8 billion, higher than the previous bar of US$3 billion. This, again, further biases the selection of companies. In many cases small companies have a much higher stock of reputational capital (i.e. they are more admired) than their larger competitors and there is no rational reason for them to be excluded from the list. *Fortune* appears to want to restrict itself to a comparison of companies that are already big enough to fit into their list of the World's 500 largest companies. Following on from the definitions introduced earlier in this paper, the *Fortune* list presents not reputations but stakeholder specific corporate images at a 'micro' level.

3.5 Seven competitive elements

For the purposes of conducting further research I have added to, extended and combined both the RQ and *Fortune's* reputational criteria to include elements that have been individually overlooked or misrepresented. A number of the elements look similar, but benefit from subtle yet essential changes in terminology. In a number of cases the term 'performance' has been replaced with 'credibility'. This is designed to acknowledge the fact that reputation is *not* necessarily fashioned by actual performance. I argue that credibility is a more appropriate term because as we have discovered reputation is based on perceived performance.

This proposal of reputational elements is just that, it is not designed to be used in the same way as the *Fortune* or Fombrun scales. It is designed to add to an acknowledged gap in the literature regarding the development of reputation theory – a foundation that is required before further work is conducted (Wartick, 2002). It does not offer any auxiliary form of rationalisation or weighting to facilitate its usage as a management tool.

The seven elements (in no particular order) identified are:

1. ***Knowledge and skills***: A company can only be as good as its employees, who are 'the' major determinant of current and future success. As drivers of innovation, the optimum use of their talent is paramount to growth.

   - Primarily covers *Fortunes* 'Employee Talent' and 'Innovation'. Partially derived from Stephen Covey's definition of a habit, that is to form a habit you need to have the necessary skill set and knowledge base (Covey, 1989).
2. ***Emotional connections***: Consumers attach emotions to services and products; without this emotional connection many companies would be alike. Includes the perceived values and culture of an organisation, and how these link with those of its stakeholders.
   - Links with Fombruns 'Emotional Appeal'. Kevin Roberts, the CEO of Saatchi-Saatchi suggests that emotional connections are one of the factors contributing to 'lovemarks'.[42]
3. ***Leadership, vision and desire***: Stakeholders attach a high value to companies that are perceived to be led by a group of people who have vision and desire. It is not enough simply to have vision, the company must be perceived as being able to realise its visions. This element refers to perceptions concerning motivated and visionary leadership; it equally refers to governance style and practice.
   - Directly refers to Fombruns 'Leadership and Vision' but also covers the non-financial aspects of Fortunes 'Long Term Investment Value'. The term desire is derived from Stephen Coveys '*The Seven Habits of Highly Effective People*'. He suggested that to be an effective individual you must have the motivation or the 'want to do' (Ibid), I argue that the same concept can be applied to companies.
4. ***Quality***: Concerns product or service quality, that is, whether a company is seen to be meeting customer's requirements, not just once but consistently. This element concerns historical reliability and examines whether the company has consistently supplied products and services of unrivalled quality.
   - Directly covered by the Fortune List and partially by 'Products and Services' from Fombruns RC.
5. ***Financial credibility***: The traditional means by which a company's performance is judged. To build credibility the company should have a strong historical and contemporary record for generating better than average returns for shareholders.
   - Covered by both the Fortune list and Fombrun's 'Reputational Quotient'. One aspect of the 'triple bottom line'.[43]
6. ***Social credibility***: This element concerns the company position within society; it examines whether the company is perceived as being a valuable actor in society, acting as a 'good citizen' and adding to social equity, therefore earning a 'licence to operate'. It can be clearly separated from environmental credibility, primarily because

the two are so often in direct conflict. Society's demands are as often aligned with financial performance as they are with environmental responsibility.
- Covered by both Fombrun's and Fortune's lists, but for differing reasons.

7. ***Environmental credibility***: In a society framed by growing environmental problems businesses need to ensure that they are not perceived to be adding to the negative legacy that we leave for future generations. Not only this, but to create maximum value the business should strive to create environmental value, thereby offsetting the actions of less responsible organisations.
   - One aspect of the 'triple bottom line' wholly neglected in both lists. Probably, and naively assumed to be included in social responsibility.

This list of elements should be considered as a useful, stand-alone hit-list of arenas within which the modern corporation will increasingly, and does currently, compete for reputational value. It is certainly not designed to be used as the basis for another commercially orientated ranking system. The obvious problem and deliberate quandary is that out of these seven elements only one is currently fully tangible – financial credibility.[44] In the majority of cases the information relating to the other elements which is key to corporate reputation lies hidden in previously uncollected non-financial information. The message being that the way to build and sustain a strong reputation is first, to collect and second, to manage non-financial information/key performance indicators (KPIs). This is on top of the existing processes and procedures in place to collect financial information.

Clearly as reputations are not necessarily built on fact, but perception, it is important to not only collect and manage this information – but also to transparently communicate it with stakeholders. As it stands stakeholders are already using their own intuition (perhaps with a little help from NGOs) to judge businesses in these seven areas, therefore it makes sense for a company to try to minimise the uncertainty and give them the information that will help them to build imagery.

At the commencement of a strategy of this nature a company may not be performing well in each of the arenas, while this is an obvious drawback – if stakeholders can be convinced that the company can, and wants to, improve (via timelines and roadmaps) then they will likely give them the benefit of the doubt – provided of course that performance then improves year on year.

To conclude, assuming that companies find suitable methods to measure and communicate their performance in all the seven elements of reputation, then theoretically good performance will be rewarded with, among other benefits, an untarnished image or an improved reputation. The benefit to a company may be immediate, but if not it will certainly be visible in the medium term. As time passes previously intangible elements of the equation are becoming more tangible (as indicators are developed), as this process continues the relative importance of each of the elements will undergo a re-shuffle. Financial information will be unlikely to become less important, but the other six elements can only grow in their potential to influence perception and therefore reputation.

3.6 Summary

Corporate or organisational imagery is a subject that will come to increasing prominence in a world where product or service differentiators are difficult to come by. The stakeholder's rules and their longstanding, dynamic opinions count. Stakeholders view corporations and organisations through a series of filters, filters that have the power to direct purchasing and investment decision-making strategies. Although this has always been the case, globalisation has changed the nature of these filters making it harder for organisations to reconcile their numerous, real-time images. Globalisation has done to the corporate world what the ocean frequently does to cliffs during storm surges; it has exposed parts that had lain concealed for a long time. *'Real time reactionism'* realised through imagery has the ability to significantly affect the earnings potential of the contemporary corporation. Depending on one's perspective this creates a significant risk or opportunity, either way it demands attention.

Element	*Abbreviation*
1 Knowledge and skills	KS
2 Emotional connections	EM
3 Leadership, vision and desire	LV
4 Quality	Q
5 Financial credibility	FC
6 Social credibility	SC
7 Environmental credibility	EC

As we have seen throughout this chapter, reputations are formed and influenced primarily by *character* and diverse *images*, both of which are in turn affected by *reputation*. The reputational cycle does not have a beginning or an end; in essence it cannot be created (unlike energy, it can be destroyed) but only influenced. I have argued that the best way to influence reputation is to look at how it is constructed and to strive to outperform the competition in seven key arenas.

Superior performance in these arenas coupled with essential transparency leads to enhanced corporate reputation and twenty-first century competitive advantage.

4
A Global CEO Survey

4.1 Survey purpose

During the spring and summer of 2002 I conducted a survey to examine the perceived future relationship between sustainability issues (as outlined in Chapter two) and the reputation of large multinational corporations (as discussed in Chapter three).

4.1.1 Brief outline

The Chief Executive Officers (CEOs) of the Global Fortune 500 (the world's largest companies – ranked by revenue) were presented with three scenarios of the future business climate. Given each individual scenario CEOs were asked to rate the seven elements of reputation (as presented in Chapter three) for their probable significance to the preservation of a positive corporate reputation (within their own company). They were then asked to return their surveys by freepost service to Cambridge for analysis. A full copy of the survey can be found in Appendix 1.

4.2 The sample

A number of different audiences could have been surveyed with respect to the purpose. To ensure that my results were of relevance I felt that it was important to ensure that the sample represented the opinions of those who plan, design and execute business models based upon the global state of affairs. Following this, my sample consists of the CEOs identified in the year 2001 (the latest version available at the time of development) version of the Global Fortune 500. At the time these leaders were making daily decisions or judgements based upon current and predicted future patterns of society and the environment.[45] In order to be precise it was important that in each case the survey had been read and completed by decision makers within their respective corporations. As the survey population was finite and predetermined I conducted a census or saturation survey, that is, a count of the whole population where the target population is also the survey population. According to Cooper and Schindler, there are two conditions under which a census is more appropriate than a survey:

- When the population is small,
- When the elements are quite different from one another (Cooper and Schindler, 1998).

These conditions were satisfied by my choice of the Fortune Global 500. The survey population is small by virtue of its name and due to its global scope, variable in nature (see Chart 4.1).
The complete sample contained:

- 154 European companies.
- 104 Japanese companies.
- 200 North American companies.
- 42 from other nations.

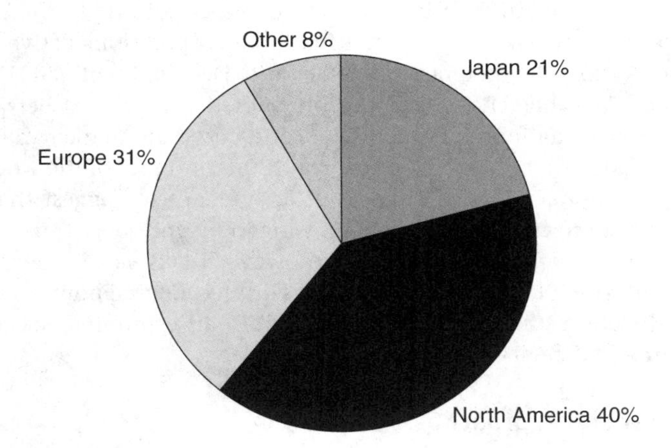

Chart 4.1 Nationality breakdown, GF500 [2001].
Source: 2001 Fortune Global 500 Database.

Although the nation of origin is an important factor, most of the companies that form the population are multinationals (with the exception of a few former state monopolies i.e. Gazprom), and by definition international in outlook. To simplify some of the key distribution and project management problems I further divided the Global Fortune 500 into three key regions (amalgamating Japan and Other): Where referred to.[46]

Europe (consists of companies headquartered in): Belgium, Britain, Finland, France, Germany, Italy, Luxembourg, Netherlands, Norway, Russia, Spain, Switzerland, Sweden.

North America (consists of companies headquartered in): USA, Canada.

OTHER (consists of companies headquartered in): Brazil, Australia, China, India, Japan, Malaysia, Mexico, Singapore, Venezuela, South Korea, South Africa.

In the year 2001 the companies surveyed provided direct employment to over 47 million people across the globe and total revenues for the group amounted to over US$14 trillion (Fortune Magazine, 2001).

4.2.1 Why large multinationals?

It is highly probable that multinational, profit-making organisations will continue to exert considerable influence over the legacy that our generation leaves for the future. Some businesses are now arguably as big and as globally influential as governments. According to the United Nations there are over 60,000 multinational corporations active today (United Nations Conference on Trade and Development, 2001). The *Financial Times* has challenged the oft quoted comparison between a country's gross national product (GNP) and corporate market value but still concluded that at least 37 of the top 100 economies of the world are corporations (Wolf, 2002). There is little evidence to suggest that this trend is about to end, in fact it is increasing in magnitude. At first glance my population appears to be small, however looks can be deceiving. This small band of corporations harbours unprecedented power over the future direction of world development, from an economic, social and environmental perspective.

4.3 Scenario approach

As we have already discovered, the survey has been designed to ascertain perceptions of the future importance of sustainability issues. Obtaining perceptions of the future is a notoriously thorny procedure. However, it is important to remember that companies, and in particular their leaders, are forced to make predictions about the future on a daily basis. They then use this information as the basis for, among other things, the direction and magnitude of investment. It is the mentality and thought processes behind these decisions that I sought to draw out.

In the past, the impact of human activity on the environment was relatively limited, relative that is to the impact that we have today. Today our decisions have consequences that reach far into the future and for this reason the future becomes of particular importance in terms of sustainability. These consequences are, in the main, uncertain both in terms of their impact and their magnitude. With this level of future uncertainty, decision makers are increasingly using different techniques to envisage the future business climate. To aid respondents thinking about the future I have employed the practice of scenario planning.

I was first introduced to this practice in 2000 by Shell. Together with Dave Knight (from Sd3) and Seb Beloe (from SustainAbility) I contributed to the development of the environmental and social aspects of their scenarios. Normally when you are being paid to give your advice as a consultant, the customers are the ones who leave the room stimulated and full of ideas, at least that is the idea. In this case I left the building full of ideas, fascinated, inspired and excited to find out more. I found the whole experience deeply liberating. Many years later after talking about this with Charles Hampden-Turner, himself a veteran of the Shell scenario team, I was told that this feeling was quite 'normal'.

A proven planning technique, 'scenario planning' has been used in the past to successfully envisage the end of the Cold War and famously for Shell, the OPEC oil crisis of the 1970s (see Schoemaker, 1995). Scenario planning does not aim to simply extrapolate current trends, it creates plausible stories of alternative futures. The 'father' of 'scenario planning', Peter Schwartz, describes scenarios as 'a tool for helping us to take a long view in a world of great uncertainty … they are stories about the way the world might turn out tomorrow' (Schwartz, 1991). The company or organisation concerned is able to use these alternate stories to 'road-test' their proposed strategies, ensuring that they are built to a robust and enduring design – regardless of actual outcome.

Scenario Planning could certainly never be described as a science. Despite this, the development of scenarios does follow a broad methodology. It primarily involves a very intensive research phase, something Schwartz termed 'Skilled Hunting' (Ibid). Researchers actively look for sources that contradict current thinking, often challenging assumptions (Ibid).

In a sense the research phase is rather like the CIA hunt for Al-Qaeda; researchers try to filter out the background noise and listen in to the less obvious signals. Scenario planning is by nature multidisciplinary. Many of the people involved with the design of scenarios are somewhat unconventional: a glance at the Global Business Network[47] website reveals among others musicians, anthropologists, economists, poets, novelists and inventors.

Once the 'less obvious signals' have been collected they are collated together with other more 'certain' driving forces to form stories. These stories have the effect of increasing understanding of the business environment, and widening traditionally constrained business horizons to potential future outcomes. These scenarios can then be used as the basis of strategic planning tools, or as the point around which high-level discussions can be held.

Summarising, the development of scenarios requires considerable expertise, resources and time. None of which were available to me. As a result I decided to turn to a set of scenarios that had already been created. In 2000 Allen Hammond, an experienced scenario planner and director of strategic analysis at the World Resources Institute (WRI), published a book entitled *Which World: Scenarios for the 21st Century*. This book contains the results of the 2050 Project, a joint research program of the Brookings Institution, the World Resources Institute, and the Santa Fe Institute. The group produced three scenarios, outlining possible worlds for the next century; 'fortress world', 'market world' and 'transformed world'.

Fortress world A vision based not only on the failure of market led growth to redress social wrongs and prevent environmental disasters but also on the belief that unconstrained markets will exacerbate these problems and that large portions of humanity will be left out of the prosperity that markets bring. These failures eventually destroy the resources and the social framework on which markets and economic growth depend. Economic stagnation spreads as more resources are diverted to maintain security and stability, as does economic fragmentation where conflict dominates or the social order breaks down. The scenario describes a future in which enclaves of wealth and prosperity coexist with widening misery and growing desperation, a future of inequality, violence, conflict and instability. (Adapted from: [*International Centre for Integrative Studies, 2000*]).

Fortress world was written before the tragic events that took place in the US on 11 September 2001. Despite this, its description resonates strongly with the kind of global environment that many pessimists predicted would occur in its wake; an environment in which security issues dominate at the expense of other less tangible concerns.

Market world This scenario describes a future based on the belief that market forces and new technology will lead to rising prosperity and will offer humanity a bright future, a future in which markets rule and global corporations dominate. Economic reform and technological innovation fuel rapid economic growth. Developing regions are integrated into the global economy, creating a powerful global market, and bringing modern techniques and products to virtually all countries. The result is widespread prosperity, peace and stability. (Adapted from: [*International Centre for Integrative Studies, 2000*]).

Market world appears to describe a post bi-polar world rather like our own, assuming that 11 September 2001 had not occurred and that the market was rather more successful at delivering social goods.

As both 'Market world' and 'Fortress world' are dominated by the behaviour of the market – albeit in very different ways – it would seem that within these scenarios, financial credibility would be of greater importance to business.

Transformed World In this scenario fundamental social and political change, and perhaps even changed values and cultural norms, give rise to enlightened policies and voluntary actions that direct or supplement market forces. 'Transformed world' envisions a society in which power is more widely shared and in which new social coalitions work from the grassroots up to shape what institutions and governments do. Democratic forms of government become almost universal and a spiritual revival triggers a surge in private philanthropy. Although markets become effective tools for economic progress, they do not substitute for deliberate social choices; economic competition exists but does not outweigh the larger needs for cooperation and solidarity among the world's peoples and for the fulfilment of basic human needs. (Adapted from: [*International Centre for Integrative Studies, 2000*]).

'Transformed world' seems to describe an idealist's solution to the world's ills. Given this global state of affairs one would assume that social and environmental issues would be higher on the agenda than in other scenarios.

As each of the three scenarios occupies a significant space in Hammond's book it would not be plausible to expect busy executives to read long texts before responding. Therefore it was decided to employ the concise scenario abstracts presented above (they were partially derived from the

International Centre for Integrative Studies report 'Cloudy Crystal Balls'). Respondents were presented with these three scenarios, one at a time. Once the respondent had read the individual shortened scenario they were asked to imagine that their company was faced with this potential operating environment. It was from within these dissimilar mindsets that respondents answered the proposed questions.

4.4 Hypothesis list

The shape and nature of the survey itself was determined by eight hypotheses. These hypotheses are grounded in the literature and practice research that went into Chapters 2 and 3.

1. European companies will rate environmental and social credibility higher than their North American and *other* counterparts.
2. Both social and environmental credibility are considered to be as important to the preservation of a positive corporate reputation (across scenarios) as quality.
3. Both social and environmental credibility will have as great an impact on the preservation of a positive corporate reputation (across scenarios) as financial credibility.
4. Environmental and Social Credibility – as elements of reputation – are appearing on the 'radar' of large global corporations. They are considered to be of significance to the preservation of a positive corporate reputation.
5. Financial institutions consider both social and environmental credibility to be more significant to the preservation of a positive corporate reputation than their peers.
6. The largest respondents (in terms of annual revenue) consider both social and environmental credibility to be more significant to the preservation of a positive corporate reputation than the smallest.
7. Financial credibility is considered to be more significant to the preservation of a positive corporate reputation within both market and fortress world than in transformed world.
8. Both social and environmental credibility are considered to be more significant to the preservation of a positive corporate reputation within transformed world than in market world.

4.5 Design

Globally, there are a limited number of surveys that attempt to engage CEOs from large multinationals, examples include: (PricewaterhouseCoopers,

2003; The Conference Board, 2002; World Economic Forum, 2002). Despite looking, I was unable to find any large-scale academic parallel. In the majority of cases CEO surveys take advantage of pre-existing relationships, between consultants and clients. In most other cases the survey is designed and distributed by a membership organisation, such as the World Economic Forum (WEF) adding to its credibility.

Being unable to take advantage of either of these special relationships I was aware from the outset that the target sample was ambitious. To achieve the kind of high-quality results that I was looking for, I decided to examine successful surveys and loosely base my design on them. Although I did not have a pre-existing relationship, I could certainly leverage on the good reputation of Cambridge University and my experience in producing high quality corporate documents.

As the institutions and/or companies currently involved with CEO surveys are generally commercially focused, their methodology is not publicly available – this unfortunate situation hampered my initial survey design. With little in the way of existing guidance I relied heavily on comprehensive pre and pilot tests. These resulted in three significant changes in both content and design. Throughout the process Hammond's scenarios remained broadly similar, although wording was slightly changed to make it more understandable to respondents who did not have English as a first language.

Within each of the three scenarios respondents were asked to rate the seven elements of reputation (as introduced in Chapter 3) for their importance to the preservation of a positive corporate reputation.

To directly tackle the potential issue of low response rates, all of the survey betas and the final product were designed to partially fulfil Dillman's (Dillman, 1978) *Total Design Methodology (TDM)*. Dillman's method focuses on attention to detail within two key areas: survey construction and survey implementation. I have used the term 'partially' because of the following issues:

- Unconventional nature of my survey,
- Completely different target audience (Dillman focused primarily on American households),
- Major advances in technology/media since publication (1978).

4.5.1 Pre and pilot tests

Before the survey was sent out in its entirety I produced and circulated both a pre and pilot test version.

Initially I had planned to do a comparative survey, looking for differences in the relationship between reputation and sustainability in two key business sectors: the transport sector and the IT sector. These two sectors were chosen because they are very different in terms of environmental impact, one being a traditionally dirty manufacturing industry, the other being perceived to have little impact on the environment. Accordingly, the pre and pilot surveys were split into three sections, according to the three scenarios, and then again each scenario section was split in two (see Figure 4.1).

Respondents were asked to imagine, not only that they were in the future, but also that they belonged to two different sectors.

The survey (Beta 1) was first subjected to a pre-test with 20 of my peers (all of whom responded), several of the group did not speak English as their first language. This process highlighted a number of small, but nevertheless important areas of reduced clarity. A second pre-test (Beta 2) was conducted among a group of 10 (from the original 20) to assess selected improvements.

Non-collaborative pilot

After the pre-test changes were made, the revamped survey was piloted (Beta 3). The pilot sample taken represented one-fifth of the total population, that is, 100 out of the population of 500. The sample was selected by taking every fifth company in the list, thereby creating a sample that reflected a broad cross section (in terms of revenue) of companies within the total population. The sample contained:

- 27 European companies or 27 per cent (overall representation in total population: 31 per cent).
- 20 Japanese companies or 20 per cent (overall representation in total population: 21 per cent).

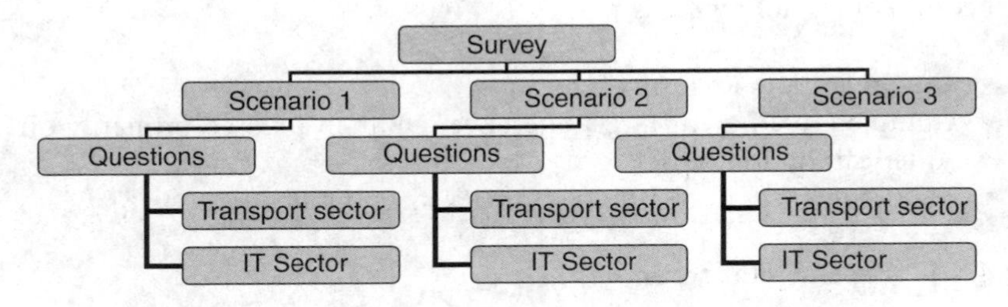

Figure 4.1 Graphic showing the structure of the pre and pilot surveys.

- 43 American Companies or 43 per cent (overall representation in total population: 37 per cent).
- 10 From Other Nations, or 10 per cent (overall representation in total population: 11 per cent).

When compared with the nationality breakdown for the entire survey population it can be seen that this selection virtually mirrors the overall population breakdown.

On 22 February 2002 the initial package containing the following four elements was finally posted:

1. Cover Letter
The initial cover letter was considered to be the most important part of the mailed package, and as Dillman suggested 'every sentence [was designed to] serve a distinct purpose' (Ibid). The letter contained a brief description of the research, outlined what the respondent stood to gain from responding, and explained how much time they might need to commit to the task.

2. Survey Booklet
In order to achieve the desired professional finish the booklet was printed in full colour by *Cambridge University Press*. I also produced an *Adobe Acrobat* electronic version to be posted on the internet.

3. Bookmark
Comments from my pre-test sample suggested that the reader may not fully understand what the seven elements of reputation meant, or what they represented. In order to tackle this I designed and printed a full colour bookmark on heavyweight card. This carried a more detailed explanation of each element.[48]

4. International Business Reply (freepost) Envelope
Despite the respondents' position within their companies (CEOs are probably not overly concerned about postage or postal costs), it was decided that to make replying as easy as possible, an International Business Reply service would be activated. The provision of reply envelopes also added an air of professionalism to the project. The Royal Mail provided me with a unique address, postcode and special electronically recognisable envelope format. This envelope was included in the package received by respondents.

Using Microsoft's mail merge function, labels were printed and affixed to the front of the envelopes. They were then sent using a premium first-class service.

After one and a half weeks I had only received four replies and realised that the next stage of the process would be critical. I followed the letter up with a short reminder, this was sent out on 6 March. The single sided A4 reminder contained an expanded section on the benefits of replying and was mailed inside a white Cambridge University branded envelope. This phase of the survey was more successful resulting in 11 replies. On 1 April (after a larger gap of nearly a month) the whole survey was re-sent to non-respondents. The survey was fronted by a new double-sided cover letter; one side being the letter text the other a simplified, pictorial guide to completion. This letter was printed in full colour on a higher grade of paper than previously used.[49] This phase of the survey resulted in ten replies, roughly the same as the previous letter. After waiting for three weeks it was decided that I should now follow up my written correspondence with a phone call. This policy is again in line with Dillman's method, as he suggests that the effectiveness of a telephone call as an additional follow-up can be significant. A further three replies were received, making the total response 28 out of 100, or 28 per cent.

Pre/pilot test – key learning points

The completion of a pilot test was invaluable; it resulted in a number of key learning points having implications for the final survey:

1. The first letter is the most important phase of a survey – in the case of the pilot test, it failed to produce the desired effect. Looking at increased responses from subsequent letters I concluded that the following techniques should be adopted:

- simplified wording,
- more concise style,
- graphical/Pictorial guide to completion,
- full Colour Printing,
- higher Grade Paper (while still being sourced from sustainable forests),
- more emphasis on key benefits of completion,
- greater personalisation – increase mail merge usage,
- leverage on Cambridge University brand,
- white envelopes with address windows and Cambridge University logo.

2. The time taken between follow-ups needed to be dramatically reduced: During the phone call round it became clear that CEOs' offices worked on a rolling two-week previous basis, that is, anything that arrived before that was considered to be historical. In general, all letters to CEOs are logged in a database and then the CEO is consulted on what course of action to take. In a large percentage of cases this involves simply not replying. However, in some cases it was clear (from speaking to the office) that the PA had made the decision unilaterally. In these cases response was still open for discussion.

- phone to ensure arrival and entry into database.
- personal contact is welcomed, in a number of cases PAs told me that they would inform the CEO of my call.
- use electronic communication where possible – see separate bullet.
- use different time/follow-up schedules for companies based in different regions.

3. Leverage on Cambridge University brand value and visually appealing design: My survey was in direct competition with those from other universities, and from a number of experienced, prestigious research companies. It was obvious after speaking to PA's that my coming from Cambridge was going to help my cause, particularly in the case of foreign companies. Several of the pilot CEOs' secretaries told me that they received literally thousands of letters each week. I decided that my letter should be designed to be as visually catchy and personal as possible.

4. Ensure that the company and CEO name's are correct prior to sending each letter, if this was wrong the survey will simply be disposed of: A number of companies in the sample had changed name since the Fortune database was published. This was primarily due to merger and/or acquisition (M and A).

The average length of time spent as CEO of a large company is short. A number of companies had changed CEO in the intervening period – leaving my letters addressed to an ex-employee. This was found to be a particular problem with American companies, less so with Japanese.

5. Use the word 'survey' or 'questionnaire' with caution – it has very negative connotations and can result in instant rejection. Alternatively emphasise that it is a research programme or study: When phoning CEOs I was not able to get past the main switchboard if I mentioned either of the words survey or questionnaire.

6. Electronic forms of communication are best for foreign companies, both in terms of speed of contact/reply and ability to interact: In many cases, when telephoned, the PA will freely give out email addresses.

The survey (in acrobat format) was easily transmitted online as an attachment.

I obtained a new email account, with a much larger storage limit.

7. Website is critical to the success of the survey: During the pilot four companies returned a downloaded version of the survey (see Figure 4.2). Equally it provides a means of verification of my work, as it is on the Cambridge University server it can be presumed to be a genuine piece of work and not industrial espionage.

During pilot period the website was visited by at least 300 people. The majority of visitors were direct hits (not directed by search engines) therefore it is highly probable that the majority of hits were linked to the survey mailing.

8. Remember that this is an international study: During the full survey I needed to take all possible steps to avoid national holidays. During the

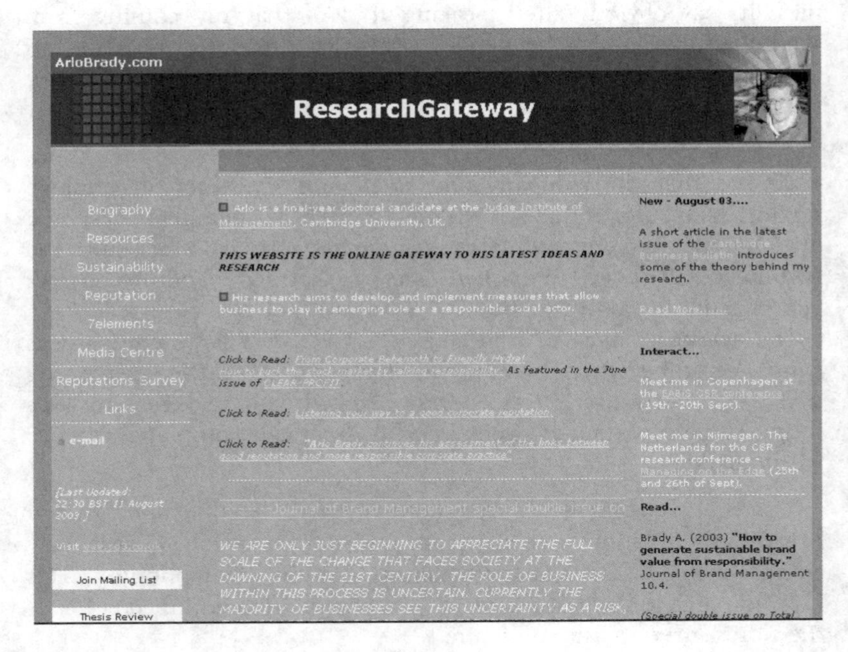

Figure 4.2 Screenshot of the project website.

pilot, I mistakenly sent the letters to Japan during a week long national holiday. The last thing that I wanted was to allow my letter to be stacked in a gigantic pile.

9. The survey needed to be as simple and easy to complete as possible, while still providing me with the required data: Following criticism during the pilot test I concluded that the comparative section of the survey should be dropped. Respondents would be asked to consider the reputational implications of each scenario on their own company. The new structure is illustrated in Figure 4.3. It was decided that the original structure was far too complicated and time consuming. Following consultation Jim Collins, the US management research 'guru', suggested that to achieve maximum response my survey should be 'simple and super, super easy to respond' (Collins, 2002). The revised survey structure took this advice into account.

10. The survey needed to guarantee respondents 'complete' confidentiality: Without full confidentiality I could not be sure that CEOs would take me beyond the boundaries of Public Relations (PR). A number of respondents questioned the confidentiality of the survey. This was despite the presence of a sentence in the covering letter outlining my policy. For the full survey a comprehensive confidentiality statement was made available online. Use of sophisticated tracking software meant that I was able to note that the statement was accessed by a large number of the respondents.

11. Respondents should be offered an incentive for completion: Dillman spoke highly of the use of incentives as a method to increase response rates, he suggested the use of a prize draw, competitions or attaching money to the survey (Dillman, 1978). Clearly in this case these types of incentives would not be appropriate. CEOs would be unlikely to be interested in tokenism; after all most of them are very

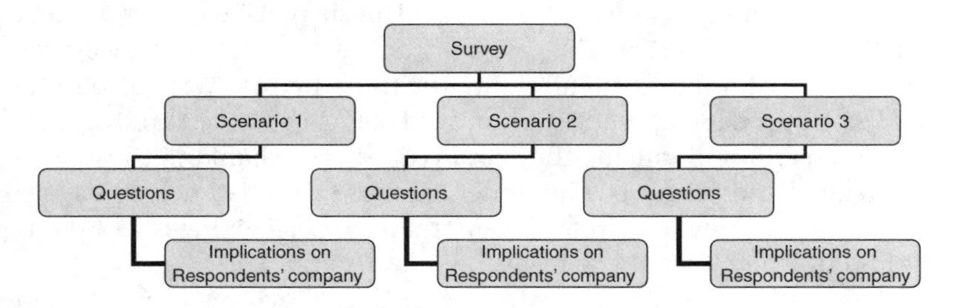

Figure 4.3 Graphic showing the structure of the final survey.

wealthy people. It was therefore decided that I could offer CEOs unique intellectual property – something that could not be already bought. Cover letters emphasised the provision of a free summary report for all interested respondents.

4.6 Timeline

The full survey was launched on Friday, 7 June 2002. This date was chosen to avoid the Queen's Golden Jubilee Celebrations. It also meant that I was able to complete the main bulk of research prior to the major summer holiday season (in continental Europe: the whole month of August plus a large number of national holidays in Japan) and avoiding the American Independence Day (4 July).

I sent out initial survey packages to each of the companies in the sample. Before each item was mailed the CEO and company name was verified using www.hoovers.com, an extremely helpful online global company database. The package informed the respondent that I would be phoning their office shortly to 'answer any questions that they may have'.

To improve manageability the 400 companies were divided into six regions:

1. UK
2. Continental Europe
3. Africa
4. America (North and South)
5. Asia
6. Oceania

I then proceeded to phone all companies in the order shown above – closest first. This process began with the UK on the 12 June, five days after the initial mailing.

Once the three week telephone/e-mail push had been completed I needed to ensure that the pressure to return did not decrease. Companies who did not refuse outright to participate were given one week from the date of their last phone call before I followed up. Together with the early respondents they received a letter, thanking those who had replied and acting as a reminder for those who had not. The letter also mentioned my incentive, the summary report – giving respondents an idea of when it would be ready.

Subsequent follow-ups were decided on a case-by-case approach and were solely restricted to those who did not reply.

4.7 Choice of statistical analysis

After the results of the survey were collated they were then placed into a *Microsoft Excel* database where they were statistically analysed to establish if the proposed hypotheses could be accepted or rejected.

In order to fulfil my confidentiality commitments it was important to ensure that it was not possible to ascertain any individual responses from the presented results. To this end, once the surveys were returned the associated company names were deleted from the record. Before this point each response was tagged with a note revealing region of origin, annual revenue and whether they were a member of the financial community. In certain cases, on its own and in combination, this information could allow the reader to determine the company concerned. Where this was deemed possible, the information was withheld. In any case the data notes were deleted after data analysis.

In the first instance, to facilitate the easy identification of trends and distribution, the data was arranged using simple descriptive statistics. Following this, a series of more in-depth techniques were employed to determine statistical significance of variance.

4.7.1 Non-parametric tests

As most frequently used statistical tests make the assumption that data comes from a normal distribution I found that the use of non-parametric tests was most appropriate (i.e. because they do not assume Gaussian distributions). The drawback of using non-parametric tests is a reduction in power to detect sample differences. However, because of my relatively large sample size this reduction in power will not be particularly evident. Because of the categorical and ordinal nature (ranked) of my data I used both the *Mann-Whitney U Test* (for un-paired data) and the *Wilcoxon signed rank sum test* (for paired data). These tests were performed using an *Excel* add-in called *Analyse-It.*[50]

Mann-Whitney U Test

The *Mann-Whitney U Test* is used to compare two independent groups of sampled data. This test calls for the data from the two independent groups to be ranked as if they were from a single population, the largest negative score receiving the highest rank. The null hypothesis being that the two groups of data are from a single population. The calculation will return a *P value*; assuming that this value is statistically significant, that is, α is less than 0.05 (5 per cent), the null hypothesis can be safely rejected.

Wilcoxon Signed Rank sum test

Like the *Mann-Whitney test The Wilcoxon Signed Rank sum test* is used to test if two populations have the same distribution. It differs because it is used to compare non-independent samples (paired).

The null hypothesis is that both distributions are the same. The test returns a P value which, if statistically significant (α is less than 0.05), can support the rejection of the null hypothesis.

4.8 Response profile

Responses were received from 269 of the 493 companies contacted. Out of these 163 companies completed the survey, representing total corporate revenues amounting to almost US$5 trillion. This equates to 34 per cent of the Global Fortune 500[51] (see Chart 4.2 that follows). Although this is not the 'best' response rate received from a business studies survey, it is important to bear in mind the type of respondents sought. Respondents of this calibre and level of influence are much more difficult to assemble than those of the general public, or indeed middle-management.

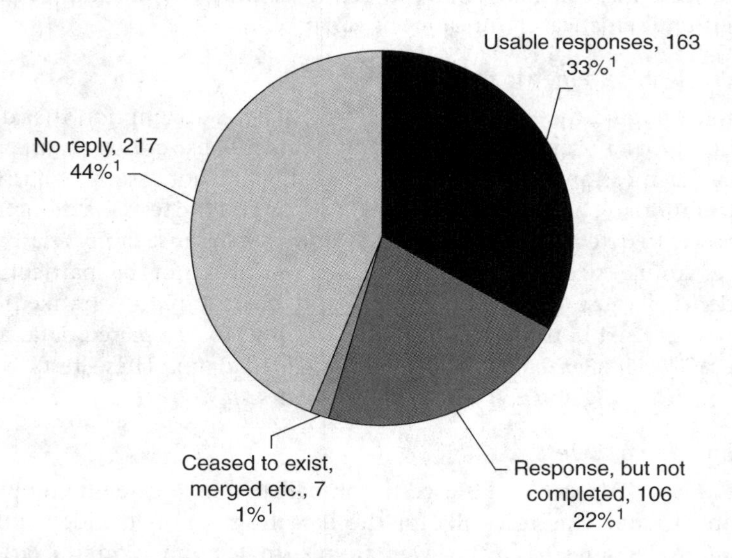

Chart 4.2 Graph showing overall (pilot[2] and full) survey response rate (n = 493).

Notes

[1] Rounded to nearest percent.

[2] Figures adjusted for discarded replies due to design change.

Sources: Own survey (2002).

It is possible that those CEOs who chose not to participate may hold very different opinions from those who did. I do not believe that this reduces the significance of the results – they still reflect the opinion of the directing-minds of a large segment of some of the largest companies in the world. With any empirical work grounded in opinion-research, the results reflect a snapshot, and there is no guarantee that respondents would answer in the same way under different circumstances.

This response profile is deliberately less 'precise' than it could be. The confidentiality clause (see Appendix 3) that I entered into with my respondents meant that I am unable to reveal a great deal of information. For example, in certain countries, or sectors, there are only a couple of GF500 companies. Given this situation, it would be relatively simple to determine individual responses from this level of information.

From the original total of 500 companies, seven had ceased to exist by the time the survey was mailed, this was discovered prior to mailing through the use of www.hoovers.com. In several cases firms had merged with other companies already in the GF500. Despite my follow-ups, 44 per cent of the companies contacted did not reply at all. Although they did not fill in the survey, 106 companies replied, either by phone, email, post or fax to say that they would not be able to participate. Also falling into this category are the responses that I received from junior/middle management.

The figures quoted in this section include several pilot replies. Although there was a design change between the pilot and full survey, it

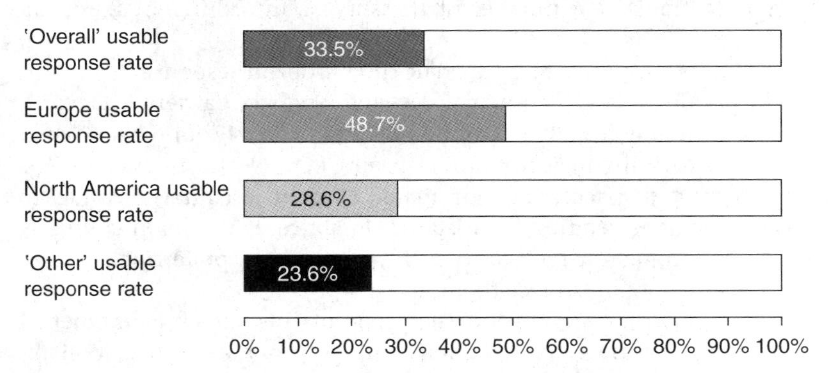

Chart 4.3 Graph showing 'usable' (pilot and full[1]) survey response rates[2] (n = 493).

Notes

[1] Rounded to nearest percent.

[2] Figures adjusted for discarded replies due to design change.

Sources: Own survey (2002).

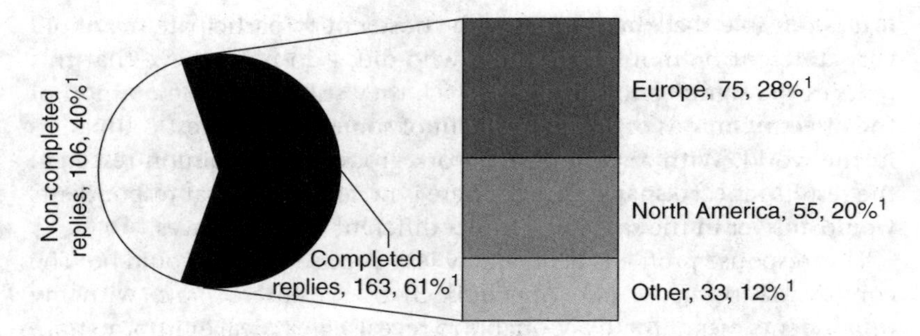

Chart 4.4 Graph showing breakdown of survey replies pull-out displays regional breakdown of completed replies[2] (n = 269).

Notes
[1] Rounded to nearest percent.
[2] Figures adjusted for discarded replies due to design change.
Sources: Own survey (2002).

was possible to salvage some pilot responses. These were exclusively responses from either companies in the IT or transport sectors.

Charts 4.3 and 4.4 show the individual response rates in their regional context. It is clear that the response from European companies was far higher than any other region. In fact, nearly 50 per cent of European companies presented a 'usable' reply. This could be attributed to the fact that I was able to spend more time eliciting responses from this region – primarily due to the similarity in time zone. Equally, I was fortunate to be able to translate a number of the surveys into different European languages.

The 'other' response rate was half the European response rate – this can be put down to difficulty of access and language barriers. The North American 'usable' response rate was 28.6 per cent. I found that, when compared with the majority of European CEOs, North American CEOs were relatively inaccessible, in many cases it was not possible to speak to their secretaries or assistants. In six cases the main company switchboard operator refused to even transfer calls, preferring to make the decision about response themselves.

For reasons that are beyond the scope of this survey a number of American CEOs are globally famous, enjoying star status (e.g. William Gates) – it was therefore difficult, if not impossible, to gain a response from many of them.

4.8.1 Financial analogues

If one is to plot the revenue distribution of the 2001 GF500 it becomes clear that there is a huge discontinuity; the large companies are very large and the smaller companies (i.e. those lower down the chart) are significantly smaller (see Chart 4.5).

I was concerned that my respondents may not represent a good spread across this distribution. For this reason I decided to compare the total revenue of respondents with the total revenue of GF500. By doing this I was able to establish the response rate expressed as a percentage of the GF500 total revenue (see Chart 4.4). At 35.5 per cent this was marginally higher than the overall response rate of 33.5 per cent; showing that on the whole the companies that replied were larger than those who did not. This is a positive result as it suggests that my respondents had a greater level of financial influence than implied by the standard response rate.

4.8.2 Improving responses

Given the same budget I believe that the response rate from this survey would have been difficult to improve upon. However, if I were to undertake a project of this nature again I would certainly employ several different techniques; although most would involve considerable extra financial aid:

- *Increased personal attention*: My respondents were not numbers, they were all very important individuals. However increased personal attention could only be fully achieved by the use of a response team, with different individuals taking responsibility for regions or sectors.

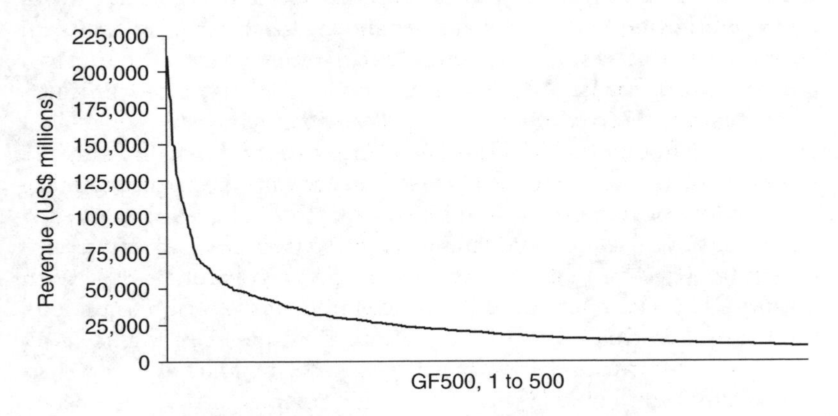

Chart 4.5 Graph showing the revenue distribution of the GF500 (n = 500).
Source: 2001 Fortune Global 500 Database.

- *Greater interactivity*: This could be achieved by making the survey fully available online, and using software that would ensure that individuals did not respond twice and so on.
- Fully translating the survey into key-languages.
- Gaining the support of one or more important individuals to *promote* the survey, preferably individuals who are likely to be admired/respected by respondents themselves.
- Offering an *in-person presentation* of the results, and customised sectoral analysis.

5
Survey Results and Conclusions*

5.1 Introduction

> This is the first time that I have seen a survey indication of differences in this area across the Atlantic.
>
> Sir Mark Moody-Stuart, Chairman AngloAmerican Plc[52]

On the 31 January 2003 the survey phase was formally closed and responses were no longer accepted. During the few months that followed the results were compiled and statistically analysed. An executive summary was published on the 10 April 2003. This summary was circulated primarily among respondents who had requested to be kept up to date, but also among other interested parties and the media.

5.2 Headline results

Chart 5.1 reveals the overall aggregate scores awarded to each element of reputation (across all three scenarios). Because the scores are averaged across differing scenarios they represent CEOs' opinions regardless of the business climate. By averaging the scores I have, in effect, put a 'damper' on outliers, extracting the underlying trends.

This revelation of scores shows that there is very little in the way of difference between the top 6 elements, the overall variation between top score and 6th score is only 0.3. A drop of this magnitude is only repeated

* NB/ To aid interpretation of the tables it is important to note that respondents were given the opportunity to score each element of reputation on a scale of 0 to 3 (0 = no significance, 1 = low significance, 2 = medium significance, 3 = high significance).

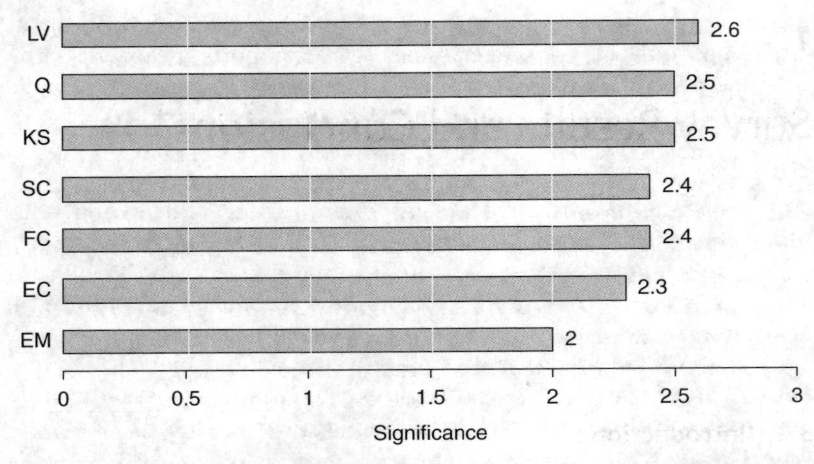

Chart 5.1 Mean significance of reputational elements (across all scenarios) (n = 269).

Notes
[1] *Figures rounded to nearest percent.*
[2] *Figures adjusted for discarded replies due to design change.*
[3] *Element abbreviations are outlined in Section 3.6.*
Sources: Own survey (2002).

at the base of the chart, separating 'environmental credibility', the last of the top 6, and 'emotional connections'.

- All seven elements of reputation received an overall score of at least medium significance to the preservation of a positive corporate reputation.
- CEOs appear to believe that six key elements will contribute most towards the preservation of a positive corporate reputation. By implication, any neglect of these key elements could result in the formation of a negative reputation. Notably, these six key elements include both 'environmental' and 'social credibility' (rated as being *individually* important).
- Perhaps without surprise global leaders conclude that 'leadership and vision' is the single most important element to the preservation of a positive corporate reputation. This is closely followed by 'quality' and 'knowledge and skills'.
- Despite recent financial scandals (Enron, WorldCom, Parmalat etc.) CEOs predict that in the near future 'social credibility' will be as important as 'financial credibility', and 'environmental credibility' will only be marginally less important.

- On average, and in virtually all of the data variations, 'emotional connections' was considered to be the least important element to the preservation of a positive corporate reputation. However, its average score suggests that it is still of medium significance.

5.2.1 By scenario

The respondents considered the importance of each element within three different scenarios. The results of this are shown in Table 5.1.

We can see considerable variation across the scenarios, for example, in different scenarios 'financial credibility' was considered to be both the *most important* and the *least important* element. 'leadership and vision', 'quality' and 'knowledge and skills' were the only elements to consistently rank in the top four. 'Emotional connections' was the only element to consistently rank in the bottom three, or achieve a score lower than 2 in any scenario.

5.2.2 Regional breakdown

The Global Fortune 500, the world's largest 500 companies by revenue, is constructed of companies from a limited regional background. To reflect this, respondents were subdivided into three clear regions of origin: Europe, North America and 'Other'.[53] Table 5.2 shows the results of the survey sub-divided into regions and averaged across all three scenarios.

Table 5.1 The seven elements of reputation in order of their perceived future impact on the preservation of a positive corporate reputation – all respondents, shown by individual scenario

Fortress world			**Market world**			**Transformed world**		
Element	**Rank**	**Score**	**Element**	**Rank**	**Score**	**Element**	**Rank**	**Score**
Financial credibility	1	2.5	Leadership and Vision	1	2.8	Social credibility	1	2.8
Quality	2	2.4	Quality	2	2.7	Leadership and vision	2	2.7
Leadership and vision	3	2.3	Knowledge and skills	=	2.7	Environmental credibility	=	2.7
Knowledge and skills	=	2.3	Financial credibility	4	2.5	Knowledge and skills	4	2.5
Social credibility	5	2.2	Social credibility	5	2.2	Quality	=	2.5
Environmental credibility	6	2	Environmental credibility	=	2.2	Emotional connections	6	2.3
Emotional connections	=	2	Emotional connections	7	1.8	Financial credibility	7	2.1

Table 5.2 The seven elements of reputation in order of their perceived future impact on the preservation of a positive corporate reputation – regional breakdown

'North America' n = 55			'Europe' n = 75			'Other' n = 33		
Element	**Rank**	**Score**	**Element**	**Rank**	**Score**	**Element**	**Rank**	**Score**
Leadership and vision	1	2.6	Leadership and vision	1	2.6	Leadership and vision	1	2.6
Quality	=	2.6	Knowledge and skills	2	2.5	Quality	=	2.6
Knowledge and skills	3	2.4	Financial credibility	=	2.5	Knowledge and skills	=	2.6
Financial credibility	4	2.3	Social credibility	4	2.4	Social credibility	4	2.5
Social credibility	=	2.3	Quality	=	2.4	Environmental credibility	5	2.4
Environmental credibility	6	2.1	Environmental credibility	=	2.4	Financial credibility	6	2.3
Emotional connections	7	1.8	Emotional connections	7	2.3	Emotional connections	7	2

The table shows us clearly that opinions on the relative importance of the seven elements vary considerably across regions. North Americans, on average, score 'environmental' and 'social credibility' lower than either Europeans or 'Others'. However, across regions, it is important to note that 'environmental and social credibility' are never, on average, considered to be of less than medium importance. Respondents from the 'Other' countries considered both 'environmental' and 'social credibility' to be on average more important than 'financial credibility'. Europeans, on average, assigned a higher score to 'financial credibility' than North Americans or 'Others'. 'Quality' was, on average, assigned a significantly higher score by North Americans and 'Others' than Europeans.

5.3 Hypothesis 5.1

Companies based in Europe are more likely to consistently rate environmental and social credibility as being more significant than their North American and 'Other' counterparts.

During data-collation, a tag was inserted together with the data to indicate the provenance of the responding company. Table 5.3 shows the variation in mean EC and SC scores across regions. At first glance, respondents from North America certainly appear to consider EC and SC to be less important than their counterparts in Europe or 'Other'.

Table 5.3 Table showing the regional variation in mean EC and SC score (across all scenarios)

	Mean SC			Mean EC		
	Europe	**North America**	**Other**	**Europe**	**North America**	**Other**
n	75	55	33	75	55	33
Mean	2.44	2.29	2.47	2.35	2.12	2.40
Median	2.33	2.33	2.33	2.33	2.33	2.33
SD	0.39	0.54	0.36	0.53	0.64	0.4

Table 5.4 The results of a Mann-Whitney test – establishing the statistical significance of the variation

Social credibility			**Reject null?**
E ≠ NA	0.2395	2-tail	
E ≠ O	0.6701	2-tail	
E ≥ NA	0.1198	1-tail	
O ≥ E	0.3350	1-tail	
O ≥ NA	0.0971	1-tail	
Environmental credibility			
E ≠ NA	0.0480	2-tail	✓
E ≠ O	0.7166	2-tail	
E ≥ NA	0.0240	1-tail	✓
O ≥ E	0.3583	1-tail	
O ≥ NA	0.0222	1-tail	✓

Table 5.4 shows the results of a Mann-Whitney U test, used to determine the significance of this result. In terms of 'social credibility' there is no significant difference between European, North American and 'Other' responses. However, European respondents rate Environmental credibility significantly higher than their North American counterparts. Other respondents also rate 'environmental credibility' significantly higher than their North American counterparts.

Using the same methodology if the European and 'Other' responses are combined and compared with the North American responses we can observe that the 2 groupings differ significantly with regard to 'environmental credibility' (Mann-Whitney U Score: 2329.5, p value: 0.033) – but not 'social credibility' (Mann-Whitney U Score: 2580.5, p value: 0.220).

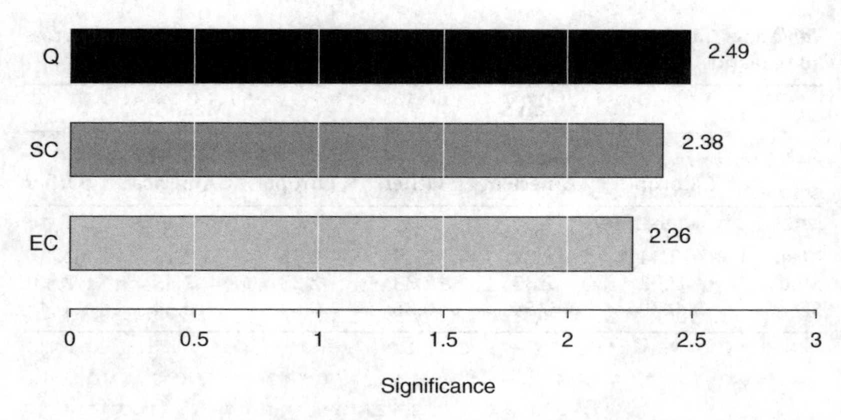

Chart 5.2 Graph showing variation in mean significance of Q, EC and SC across all scenarios (n = 163).

Significance key: High (3), Med (2), Low (1), None (0).

Sources: Own survey (2002).

5.4 Hypothesis 5.2

Both social and environmental credibility are as significant to the preservation of a positive corporate reputation (across scenarios) as quality.

Chart 5.2 shows a comparison between the mean score assigned to all three elements (EC, SC and Q) concerned. By looking at this chart we can see that there is apparent variation between each element. On average, CEOs clearly consider 'Quality' to be more significant to the preservation of a positive corporate reputation than either environmental or social credibility [see Table 5.5].

To establish if the hypothesis could be rejected, I conducted a Wilcoxon Signed Ranks test. As Table 5.6 shows, this revealed that Quality is perceived to be *significantly* (at 5 per cent) more important (across scenarios) than EC or SC.

5.5 Hypothesis 5.3

Both social and environmental credibility are as significant to the preservation of a positive corporate reputation (across scenarios) as financial credibility.

Chart 5.3 shows a comparison between the mean score assigned to all three elements (EC, SC and FC) concerned. By looking at this chart we

Table 5.5 Data table for Chart 5.2

Social credibility Mean	2.38
SC median	2.33
SC SD	0.45
Environmental credibility mean	2.26
EC median	2.33
EC SD	0.55
Quality mean	2.49
Q median	2.67
Q SD	0.44

Table 5.6 The results of a Wilcoxon Signed Ranks test – establishing the statistical significance of the variation

	SC ≠ Q	**Reject null?**
2-tailed *p*	0.0155	✓
	EC ≠ Q	
2-tailed *p*	< 0.0001	✓
	Q ≥ SC	
1-tailed *p*	0.0078	✓
	Q ≥ EC	
1-tailed *p*	< 0.0001	✓

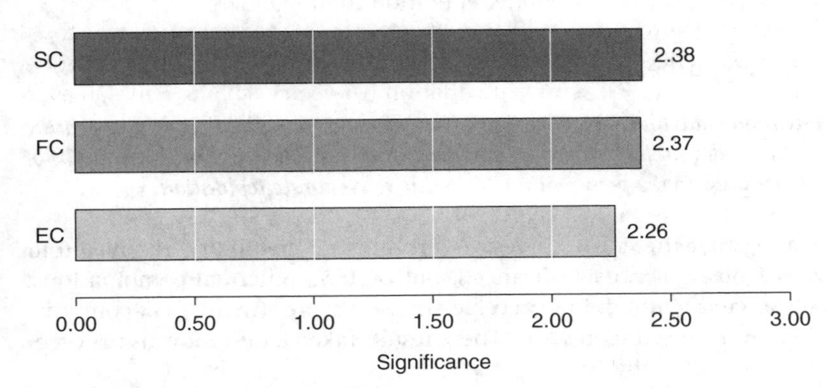

Chart 5.3 Graph showing variation in mean significance of EC, SC and FC across scenarios (n = 163).

Significance key: High (3), Med (2), Low (1), None (0).

Sources: Own survey (2002).

Table 5.7 The results of a Wilcoxon Signed Ranks test – establishing the statistical significance of the variation

	FC ≠ EC	Reject null?
2-tailed *p*	0.0300	✓
	FC ≥ EC	
1-tailed *p*	0.0150	✓
	FC ≤ EC	
1-tailed *p*	0.9850	
	FC ≠ SC	
2-tailed *p*	0.9260	
	FC ≤ SC	
1-tailed *p*	0.5370	
	FC ≥ SC	
1-tailed *p*	0.4630	

can see that there is little variation between FC, SC and EC is only marginally behind.

Using the Wilcoxon Signed Ranks test[54] we can establish whether the observed difference between mean scores is significant.

Table 5.7 shows that FC is as significant (at 5% level, cross scenario) as SC. However, the relationship between FC and EC appears to be somewhat different; FC is in fact more significant (at 5 per cent) to the preservation of a positive corporate reputation than EC.

5.6 Hypothesis 5.4

Environmental and Social Credibility – as elements of reputation – are appearing on the 'radar' of large multinational corporations. They are considered to be of significance to the preservation of a positive corporate reputation.

Throughout the entire survey 'environmental credibility' received four zero scores (or 'no significance'), out of 1633 potential combinations. 'social credibility' did not receive any zero scores (in all 1633 combinations SC received scores ≥1). These results taken alone allow us to accept the stated hypothesis.

This conclusion is supported by Table 5.8, showing that respondents, on average, consistently rated environmental and social elements of reputation as being certainly 'of significance' (that is a score of 1 or above), regardless of scenario. On average, both EC and SC achieved scores of > 2 (that is > 'medium significance'), in certain circumstances

Table 5.8 Average scores for EC and SC (NB. Figures may not add up due to rounding) [n = 163]

	Overall	FW	MW	TW
Environmental Credibility Mean	2.26	2.11	2.10	2.63
EC SD	0.55	0.7	0.75	0.58
EC Median	2.33	2	2	3
Social Credibility Mean	2.38	2.24	2.14	2.81
SC SD	0.45	0.69	0.65	0.44
SC Median	2.33	2	2	3

Table 5.9 Data table for Chart 5.4

	Financial institutions (n = 43)	Other institutions (n = 120)
Social Credibility Mean	2.45	2.33
SC Median	2.33	2.33
SC SD	0.38	0.47
Environmental Credibility Mean	2.38	2.26
EC SD	0.53	2.33
EC Median	2.33	0.56

(for example within transformed world) their importance was deemed to be considerably greater.

5.7 Hypothesis 5.5

Financial institutions consider both social and environmental credibility to be more significant to the preservation of a positive corporate reputation than their peers.

During data-collation a tag was inserted together with the data in order to indicate whether the respondent's company was in the financial sector.[55] Using this information Table 5.9 and Chart 5.4 were constructed, comparing mean EC and SC scores.

The table and chart show that on average respondents from the financial community assigned a marginally higher level of significance to EC and SC than respondents from other sectors. Table 5.10 shows the results of a Mann-Whitney U test – used to establish the significance of this result – neither of the null hypotheses can be rejected at the 5 per cent level.

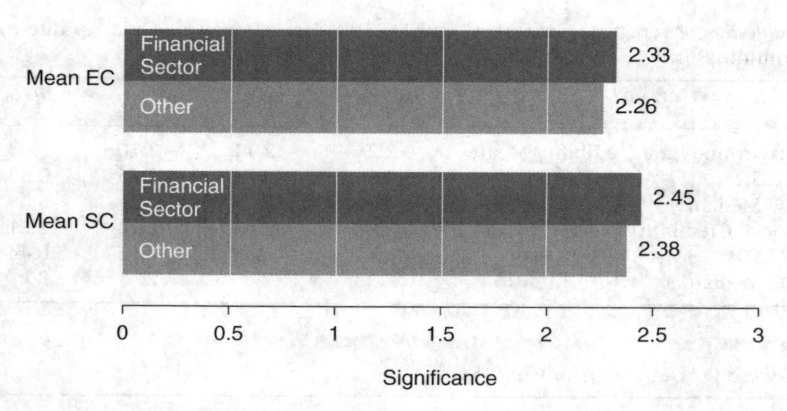

Chart 5.4 Graph showing variation in overall (cross-scenario) environmental and social scoring: Financial sector v. other sectors (n = 163).

Significance key: High (3), Med (2), Low (1), None (0).

Sources: Own survey (2002).

Table 5.10 The results of a Mann-Whitney test – establishing the statistical significance of the variation

	EC	Reject null?	SC	Reject null?
2-tailed p	Financial sec ≠ Other 0.6249		Financial sec ≠ Other 0.5179	
1-tailed p	Financial sec ≥ Other 0.3124		Financial sec ≥ Other 0.2590	

5.8 Hypothesis 5.6

The largest respondents (in terms of annual revenue) consider both social and environmental credibility to be more significant to the preservation of a positive corporate reputation than the smallest.

During data-collation, a tag was inserted together with the data to indicate the 2001 revenue of the responding company. By plotting mean score (across all scenarios for both EC and SC) against annual revenue and inserting a trend line we are able to examine the direction of the relationship (see Charts 5.5 and 5.6). Assuming that there was little or no difference in attitude we could expect the trend line to be horizontal – assuming that the hypothesis was correct we would expect to see the trend line increasing towards the right.

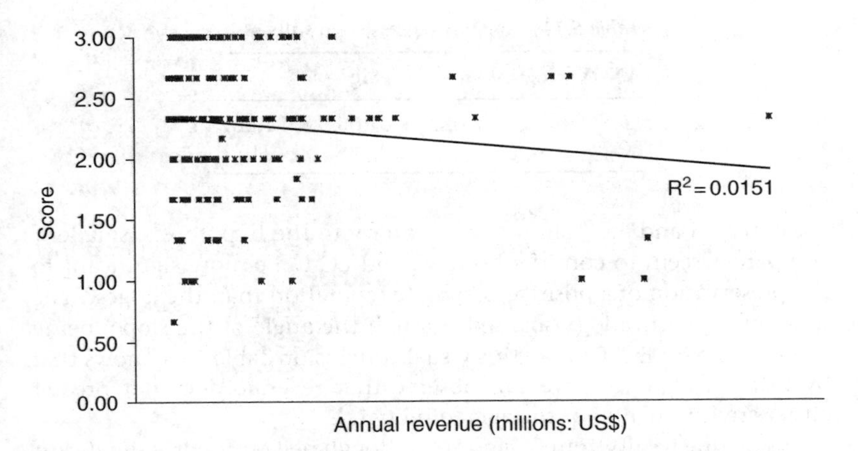

Chart 5.5 Mean EC score plotted against annual revenue (US$) with trend line (n = 163).

Significance key: High (3), Med (2), Low (1), None (0).

Sources: Own survey (2002), 2001 Fortune Global 500 Database.

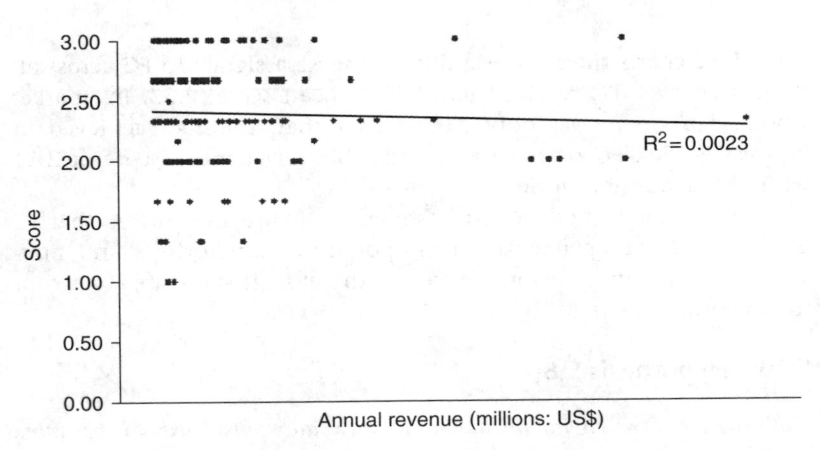

Chart 5.6 Mean SC score plotted against annual revenue (US$) with trend line (n = 163).

Significance key: High (3), Med (2), Low (1), None (0).

Sources: Own survey (2002), 2001 Fortune global 500 Database.

Table 5.11 ANOVA regression results

ANOVA regression	Sig	F
EC	0.105	2.661
SC	0.885	0.021

Charts 5.5 and 5.6[56] show that, contrary to the hypothesis, smaller[57] companies seem to consider both SC and EC to be more significant to the preservation of a positive corporate reputation than the largest. The difference in attitude (visualised through the angle of the slope) being most visible for EC. Despite this visual conclusion Table 5.11 shows that by using a regression we can observe that revenue does not predict either environmental or social credibility.

Comparing results from EC and SC, although neither result is significant the model (i.e. the idea that revenue causes changes in either SC or EC) accounts for relatively more variation in EC (i.e. is closer to significance at 5 per cent) than it does in SC.

5.9 Hypothesis 5.7

'Financial credibility is considered to be more significant to the preservation of a positive corporate reputation within both market and fortress world than in transformed world.'

Table 5.12 charts the mean significance score assigned to FC across all three scenarios. FC received its highest mean score, 2.53, in 'market world'. This score was only 0.06 greater than the 2.47 achieved in 'fortress world'. FC received a considerably lower mean score of 2.11 within 'transformed world'.

The Wilcoxon Signed Ranks test shown in Table 5.13 confirms that FC is *significantly* (at 5 per cent) more important within 'fortress' and 'market world' than in 'transformed world', therefore it is possible to accept the hypothesis as valid.

5.10 Hypothesis 5.8

'Both social and environmental credibility are considered to be more significant to the preservation of a positive corporate reputation within transformed world than in market world.'

As Table 5.14 shows, on average, CEOs assigned a markedly higher level of significance to EC and SC within 'transformed world' than in 'market

Table 5.12 Mean significance scores for FC across all three scenarios (n = 163)

	Fortress world	Market world	Transformed world
Financial credibility mean	2.47	2.53	2.11
FC SD	0.61	0.54	0.64
FC median	3	3	2

Table 5.13 The results of a Wilcoxon Signed Ranks test – establishing the statistical significance of the variation

	FW ≠ MW	Reject null?
2-tailed *p*	0.3698	
	FW ≠ TW	
2-tailed *p*	<0.0001	✓
	MW ≠ TW	
2-tailed *p*	<0.0001	✓
	FW ≥ TW	
1-tailed *p*	<0.0001	✓
	MW ≥ TW	
1-tailed *p*	<0.0001	✓

Table 5.14 Data table showing variation in perceived significance of SC and EC with two scenarios (n = 163)

	Market world	Transformed world
Social credibility mean	2.16	2.82
SC median	2	3
SC SD	0.65	0.44
Environmental credibility mean	2.15	2.65
EC median	2	3
EC SD	0.75	0.58

world'. Within 'market world' SC and EC appear to have received similar scores, however in 'transformed world' SC and EC received quite different mean scores – although both were subject to an increase. The largest increase in perceived significance of all seven elements was attained by

Table 5.15 The results of a Wilcoxon Signed Ranks test – establishing the statistical significance of the variation

	EC		**SC**	
	TW ≠ MW	**Reject null?**	**TW ≠ MW**	**Reject null?**
2-tailed *p*	<0.0001	✓	<0.0001	✓
	TW ≥ MW		TW ≥ MW	
1-tailed *p*	<0.0001	✓	<0.0001	✓
	TW ≤ MW		TW ≤ MW	
1-tailed *p*	1.0000		1.0000	

SC, going from a mean score of 2.16 in 'market world' to 2.82 in 'transformed world' – an increase in significance of 0.66.

A Wilcoxon Signed Ranks test confirms that EC and SC are perceived to be *significantly* (at 5 per cent) more important within 'transformed world' than in 'market world' (see Table 5.15).

5.11 Survey conclusions

The primary objective of this research, as the title suggests, was to establish the future impact that sustainability issues are likely to have on the reputation of MNCs; thus contributing to the current debate about the nature and strength of corporate sustainability drivers (as outlined in Chapter 2).

This was a difficult question because, if one were to be brutally honest, in the future, almost anything could happen. The difference between this research and other 'future based' research is that the information that I was looking for was camouflaged. I was looking for an insight into the way that CEOs felt that they should be currently approaching sustainability issues.

Responses to the survey have revealed how the directing minds of some of the largest companies in the world would like to approach the future. Differently from an interview on the television, or in a magazine, the anonymity associated with this survey meant that CEOs were under no obligation to say the 'right thing'; they were instead free to 'speak' their mind. In essence, the research revealed high-level speculation as to the future importance of EC and SC; speculation that is an ongoing, necessary and formative part of corporate strategy development.

In Chapter 3, I went some way to establishing the value of corporate imagery to a large business. With this as context, the empirical evidence

I have gathered now allows me to argue that in the near future CEOs of large MNCs expect EC and SC to play an important role in maintaining a positive corporate reputation.

On average, I discovered that CEOs believe that SC will be at least as important as FC. This finding taken alone should automatically act as a wakeup call for sustainability disbelievers and clearly represents the most significant finding of the survey. It shows that even CEOs (considered by many to parody and embody the worst aspects of capitalism, see: *The Economist*, 2002) are aware that the time has come for business to acknowledge its environmental and social responsibilities, citing reputation as the primary driver for behavioural change. This finding also resonates with, and strongly reinforces,[58] the key finding of a WEF global CEO survey undertaken in 2002; this concluded that 'business leaders around the world are under growing pressure to demonstrate outstanding performance not only in terms of competitiveness and market growth, but also in their corporate governance and corporate citizenship' (World Economic Forum, 2002). The WEF went further and predicted that 'the linkages between competitiveness, governance and citizenship – at the level of both the firm and the nation – are likely to grow stronger and to become more crucial to the agenda of both public and private sector leaders' (Ibid).

United States President George W. Bush recently noted in reference to 11 September 2001 that 'after America was attacked, it was as if [the] entire country looked into the mirror and saw [their] better selves. *We* were reminded that *we* are citizens, with obligations to each other, to our country, and to history. *We* began to think less of the goods we can accumulate, and more about the good that *we* can do' (George W. Bush, 2002). This heralded attitude change is perhaps not yet as apparent as President George Bush fervently described. However I would argue that that change is occurring (perhaps the drivers are a little different) and it is certainly not restricted to American citizens. A recent global public opinion survey concluded that the 'last year has shown a surge in the proportion of consumers that report having punished a company they perceive as socially irresponsible. This trend is particularly pronounced

Proposition 5.1

In the near future EC and SC are predicted to play an important role in maintaining a positive corporate reputation.

in industrialized countries' (Environics Ltd, 2003). By their responses to my survey, it appears that CEOs' perceptions are in line with public opinion and that they certainly envisage some serious value changes taking place among stakeholders in the near future. It is important to note that the changes that we can expect to see are not mutually exclusive; CEOs do not predict that environmental and social issues will eclipse financial or other associated issues – but complement them. This harmonisation of focus between financial profits and other extraneous issues is something that *visionary* companies have arguably been attempting to practice for many years (Collins and Porras, 1994). For example, in the mid-nineties Collins and Porras' prominent study concluded that 'profitability is a necessary condition for existence and a means to more important ends, but it is not the end in itself … . Profit is like oxygen, food, water, and blood for the body; they are not the point of life, but without them, there is not life' (Ibid).

For millennia, scientists, philosophers, anthropologists and others have sought to explain and understand the meaning of life. However, no one has ever succeeded in doing so. This is because the natural world and life itself are so inherently complex. As businesses grow in size and influence, they are also becoming increasingly complex (Lissack *et al.*, 1999) mimicking nature (Benyus, 1997). In a society where we are bombarded by information, complexity is becoming commonplace (see Arthur, 1999). This very complexity calls for a different approach to dilemma resolution: Integration, the essence of sustainability (balancing sometimes conflicting interests).

My results suggest that in order to extract advantage from intangibles, business will need to learn to manage this very complexity. Success will only likely be achieved through the balanced management of competing issues. We discovered in Chapter 2 that from the sustainability perspective it is not helpful to view any of the issues associated with the TBL individually. This is the primary downfall of John Elkington's TBL model. To illustrate the complex dilemmas and trade-offs inherent to sustainability I argue that it would be more useful to adopt a model based on Forum for the Future's 'five capitals' approach (as introduced

Proposition 5.2

In the near future EC and SC will be of importance to the preservation of a positive corporate reputation, not individually but as part of a broad spectrum of interrelated issues (see the other elements of reputation).

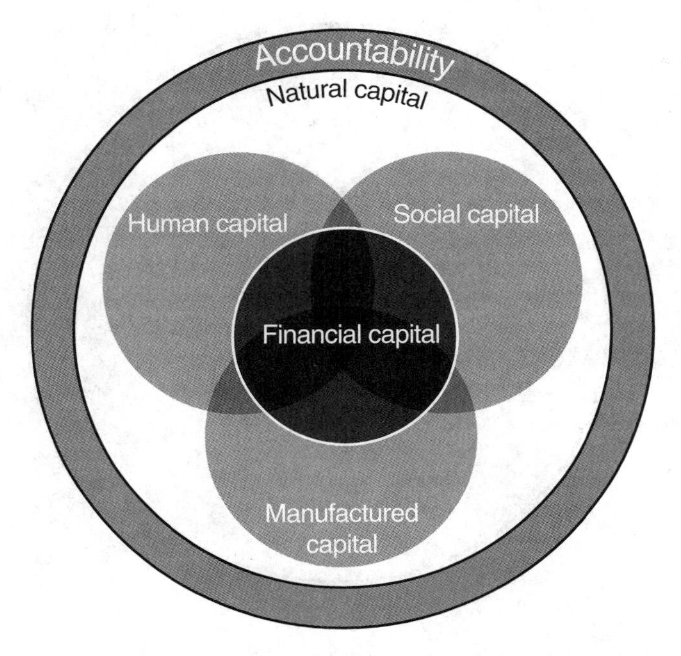

Figure 5.1 Diagram showing the relationship between each of the 'five capitals' (British Standards Institution, 2003).

in Chapter 2). By utilising a Venn diagram observers are better placed to discern the symbiotic relationship between each of the primary issues.

Figure 5.1 builds on the 'five capitals' model and highlights Collins and Porras' point that 'financial capital is critical to the ongoing survival of an organisation' (British Standards Institution, 2003). Nevertheless, because of the level of integration and overlap, financial capital is also dependant on the success of the other four capitals. The wider circle of accountability is supposed to represent the relationship of the company with its stakeholders – suggesting, helpfully, that we are still dealing with perceptions and not necessarily reality.

Re-elaborating on this diagram we can demonstrate the evident relationship between the five capitals and the seven elements of reputation (as introduced in Chapter 3).

The results of my survey coupled with the message conveyed by Figure 5.2 shows that, on the whole, CEOs predict that aspects of corporate reputation corresponding to each of the 'five capitals' will contribute strongly towards the preservation of a positive corporate

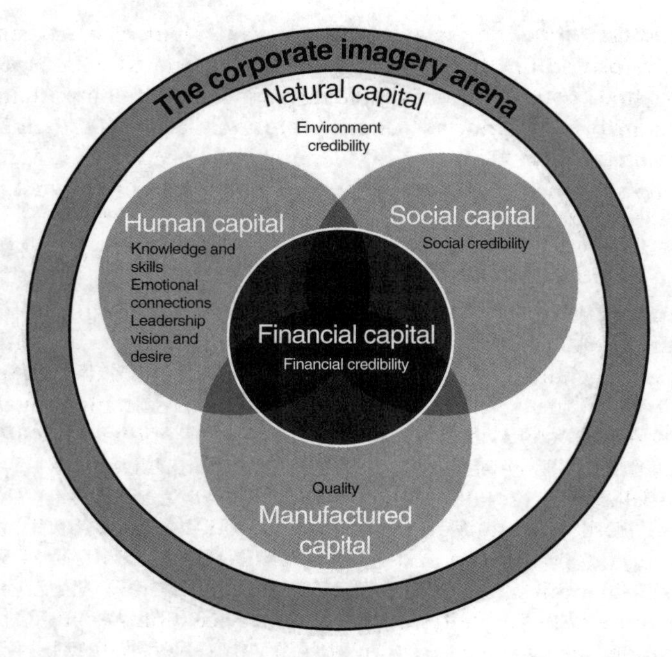

Figure 5.2 Diagram showing the relationship between each of the 'five capitals' and the 'seven elements of reputation' (adapted from British Standards Institution, 2003).

reputation – and, by implication, the creation of competitive advantage. Technically speaking, if a company is able to increase stocks of its capitals and live off the interest that they provide, it will also be able to benefit from a corresponding growth in intangible value. But this is not the whole story, as we have shown in Chapter 3; it is through the imagery that surrounds the seven elements that corporations will be held accountable for their performance. Thus, companies do not just need to concentrate on increasing capital stocks, they also need to actively attempt to close the gap between performance and credibility.

This discussion is continued in section 6.1.3 entitled: 'Effective performance communication.'

5.12 The other elements

The survey revealed a great deal of interpretable information. As a matter of fact, in itself, such a wealth of information could inform a number of books. Out of the original seven elements of reputation, my analysis has only focused on those elements closely associated with the triple bottom line. My focus does not remove from the importance of other comparisons; indeed perhaps future analysis will draw some conclusions.

Having said that, it is worth spending some time briefly looking at each of the elements that have not been closely interpreted.

5.12.1 Emotional credibility

Standing back from the respective importance of FC, EC and SC we can see that in total contrast with current thinking about the construction of corporate reputation, emotional connections are not expected to play a major role in the construction of future reputations. In his annual *Wall Street Journal* article, Alsop for example classifies emotional appeal as 'the primary driving force behind corporate reputation' (Alsop, 2002) – if we are to believe the results of this survey, this is expected to change. Drawing from the results of this research I would suggest that in an era of advanced globalisation and greater connectivity, emotional connections will be less resolute and more susceptible to factual input. Perhaps in the future rather than 'resting on good service' (Ibid) reputations will be grounded in perceived performance. In this eventuality, MNCs will need to adapt to a new role for PR, as the endgame, only to be utilised after real changes have been implemented.

5.12.2 Leadership, vision and desire

Leadership is one of the most enduring, universal human responsibilities (Kanter, 1996). History teaches us that in order for a company, government, club or any other gathering of people to succeed in its aims it is important to have a strong, charismatic (Weber, 1947) and visionary figurehead (Nanus, 1995). Bennis concurs, suggesting that it is also critical for a leader to espouse a 'strongly defined sense of purpose'. But this is not the whole story, effective leadership is about more than just words, it is about living the vision, day in day out (Bennis, 1997; Roddick, 1992).

My research suggests that public perception of this leadership style will be the single most important factor influencing overall corporate reputation in the future.

Research conducted in Germany suggests that this is already the case: Burson-Marsteller asked opinion-leaders to evaluate the level of importance that the image of the 30 DAX-CEOs[59] contributed to the reputation of the entire company. The result suggested that the public reputation of the company is to almost two-thirds determined by its leader. Of the people surveyed 48 per cent admitted to be highly influenced by the reputation of the CEO when buying stock (TNS Emnid, 2001). In addition a further Burson-Marsteller study (this time based in the United States) of 1155 key stakeholders found that the reputation of the CEO contributes heavily to how companies are perceived today. They concluded that nearly half (48 per cent) of a company's reputation should be attributed to a CEO's reputation. The companion survey among influential stakeholders in the UK confirms the American findings with 49 per cent attributed to the CEO (Burston-Marsteller, 2001). This discussion is continued in Section 6.2 entitled: Leadership for sustainability.

5.12.3 Quality

'Doing things right first time' was the mantra of corporate America and Europe in the 1990s. According to my survey, meeting customer requirements and doing things right first time will remain of primary importance well into the future. Interestingly, the concepts of quality and sustainability have a number of things in common. Both imply that a company should adopt a more communicative stance, listening and reacting to stakeholder demands – albeit on different levels. Assuming that customers continue to demand products that are produced in an environmentally and socially acceptable manner, some of the key sustainability issues have the potential to become quality issues.

The perceived importance of quality (overall joint second place) should not come as a great surprise: over the past 20 years quality has become an indispensable and universally acknowledged element of competitive advantage. Philip Crosby's suggestion that quality could well be 'a source of profit for your company' (Crosby, 1979a) was to prove accurate. As a result he developed the concept of TQM. In the 1980s Motorola took this further and developed their 'Six Sigma System', aimed at improving the quality of organisational processes and products to a level of 3 defects per million – the 'six sigma' level of quality. Since then many other high profile companies have adopted this technique to great acclaim (Jack Welch's General Electric being a prime example).

> Proposition 5.3
>
> Public perception of leadership style will be the single most important factor influencing overall corporate reputation in the future.

Although the Western concept of quality has its origins in North America, in reality much of Japan's post-war success has been attributed to their adoption of quality and lean production techniques – known as *Kaizan*. It is therefore not a great shock to note the cross regional variation in scoring; following my survey, we can see that European CEOs consider quality to be less important in maintaining a positive corporate reputation than North Americans and 'Others'.

5.12.4 Knowledge and skills

There is much evidence to suggest that what was fleetingly titled the 'new economy' in fact refers to the 'knowledge economy' (Leadbeater, 2000; Mokyr, 2002; Stewart, 2001). Increasingly we are seeing the development of whole industries whose major product is knowledge itself, and there are also subsidiary industries whose purpose is simply to convey or manage knowledge. These initially small industries have experienced growth to the extent that they now make up a substantial portion of the global economy; this has coincided with a rapid growth of net intangible capital.

In my survey, CEOs concluded that knowledge and skills were of critical importance to the preservation of a positive corporate reputation; coming in joint-second place behind leadership, CEOs clearly understand the significant potential importance of this key intangible in the near future. This importance is reflected by the prominence given to 'human capital' in the 'five capitals' model introduced in Chapter 2.

6
Strategic Implications

6.1 New rules for the new economy

'New rules for the new economy' has been the punch line of many business publications authored by leading thinkers and researchers in the last few years (Kevin Kelly, 1998; OECD, 2000). However, following the collapse of the IT bubble many of these purported changes have not come to fruition. The old neo-liberal economic rules appear to have lingered relatively unscathed (Douglas *et al.*, 2001; Cooper, 1997). A high level expert study (Eustace, 2000) conducted under the auspices of the European Commission (EC) investigated some of these issues and concluded that while the rules may stay the same, what will undoubtedly change is the way that companies build and extract value. The EC group and other researchers have suggested that, in the future, we will see companies striving to focus more specifically on the management of intangible assets (Brookings Institution, 2000; Eustace, 2000; Hand and Lev, 2003). The EC group reminded us that intangibles are not an entirely new concept but, differently from the past, 'today a firm's intangible assets are often the key element in its competitiveness' (Eustace, 2000).

Following the results of my survey, large MNCs should be aware that on average and in a variety of different scenarios, sustainability issues have the potential to sustain and add to the intangible value of their company. As various studies go as far as to ascribe up to 70 per cent of a company's value to its intangible assets (Grey, 2001) it is not an advantage to be ignored. If companies accept this thesis, then it would be sensible to also acknowledge the converse argument – that is, that the mismanagement of sustainability issues can contribute to the erosion of intangible value. Yet, until now the debate about corporate sustainability has tended to focus almost entirely on the tangible benefits that it can bring (eco-efficiency, etc.). My research has shown that the debate must now be re-focused on to fully account for the complete impact of sustainability issues on business. This finding resonates with one of the key conclusions of the influential Turnbull Report on corporate governance. The report concluded that by December 2000 companies listed in the UK should have considered threats to their reputation every bit as rigorously as other more commonly accepted risks, that is, financial (The Institute of Chartered Accountants, 1999).

Following this conclusion, large MNCs are presented with three stark choices (see Figure 6.1). First, they can continue business as usual – that is the 'head in sand-ostrich approach' (not an option for UK-listed MNCs as would otherwise contravene the Turnbull recommendations); they can choose to do the minimum possible – thereby avoiding risk; or they can 'grab the bull by the horns' and attempt to create competitive advantage (these options are discussed in detail in the following section).

As intangible value is potentially infinite in either direction (Brady, 2003) a decision to follow 'strategy one' is indeed very risky. In fact, as Arthur Anderson discovered in 2001 – intangible value can potentially

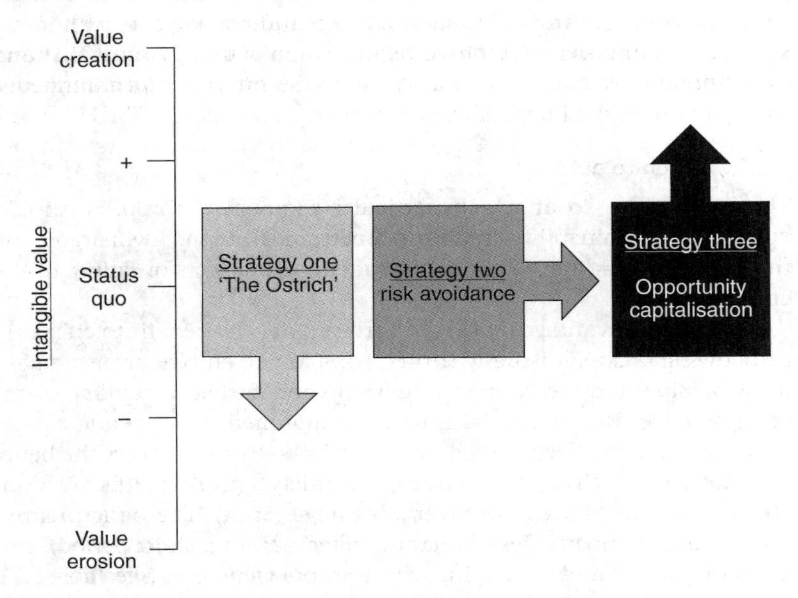

Figure 6.1 Three future intangible value strategies for MNCs.

destroy an entire company. Even if corporate leadership does not subscribe to the argument that companies should be responsible to all their stakeholders, they still have an acknowledged responsibility to their investors to ensure the longevity of their company (Friedman, 1963). My survey suggests that whether companies like it or not, in order to at least maintain a good reputation, all MNCs should plan to engage in sustainability issues in the near future – the debate about ethics and motivation, which is holding up accomplishment, should be put on the back burner. As the proverb goes, actions are stronger than words.

Earlier in this book, I introduced a diagram entitled 'the virtuous responsibility circle' (see Figure 2.8); through revisiting and expanding on this diagram it is possible to illustrate a potential way forward for companies. By combining this diagram with some of the findings of Chapter 3, I argue that sustainable positive corporate imagery is a process by-product and not something that can be created in its own right. Following this train of thought, it is not reputation that needs to be managed *per se* but the process by which it is formed. As argued in Chapter 3, the process of reputation (macro image) creation is intimately linked with corporate performance – primarily in seven areas (see the seven elements of reputation). It is this performance that is the source of all images of the corporation (both micro and macro). Over time these images pass through a series of filters and are ultimately altered. I suggest that in order to improve reputation, a company must first and most importantly, improve performance, and second, attempt to influence the structure of the image filters.

6.1.1 When to act?

The question as to at which particular moment a company should engage in a sustainability strategy is a pertinent one. As I will argue, the timing itself could have a strong impact on the success or failure of the chosen strategy.

First mover advantage (FMA) is clearly a potential benefit to engaging early in sustainability issues. The first company to engage in sustainability is possibly best positioned to develop and sustain a reputation for good practice. However, in this case the argument is academic as first moves have already been made. Not all is lost – In recent years the benefits associated with FMA have undergone criticism (Collins, 2000; Rigdon, 2000) in favour of second mover advantage (SMA). The basic premise being that a company lies dormant (strategy 2) for a short period, simply avoiding risk and complying with the applicable laws (see Table 6.1). From this position of relative safety, it allows a competitor to move first,

Table 6.1 Potential risk profile for the three response strategies

	Strategy 1	**Strategy 2**	**Strategy 3**
Short-term consequences	High Risk Possibly losses, certainly no advantage	Low Risk Zero growth	Medium Risk Possibly losses, possibly advantage
Long-term consequences	High Risk Probably losses certainly no advantage	Medium Risk Zero growth, possibly losses	Low Risk No losses, probably advantage

making and being punished for the inevitable teething mistakes. It then emerges from the sidelines having learnt from the other company's mistakes and ready to compete with advantage. In terms of sustainability a number of large companies have made their moves and their mistakes (Shell being one of the better examples). Following this model, the time has now come for companies on the sidelines (the laggards) to make their move – fully capitalising on SMA.

Following the results highlighted in Chapter 5, it would seem that one strong argument in favour of adopting 'strategy 1' is that my research was set in the future – thus removing the need to act with immediate effect. However, this conclusion is misplaced. As I argued in Chapter 3, reputations cannot be constructed overnight, they take many years to build. As a result when the future arrives it is potentially too late to alter the imagery surrounding a business.

Returning to the three drivers of corporate sustainability (Must, Could and Should) outlined in Chapter 2[60] my research has shown that the relative importance of each driver is clear. I have demonstrated that appropriate laws can act as a stimulus for innovation and they can also force laggards into action. The influence of morality as a driver should not be underestimated but equally, as the Enron case shows us, it is not to be relied upon. The 'could' argument is likely to offer corporations the maximum return on investment. However, as Table 6.1 shows this benefit does not come without exposure to considerable risk. In order to extract advantage, business needs come to terms with its role as an inclusive part of society; if it contributes towards common societal goals then it is likely to be allowed to derive benefit (in terms of profit) from it.

In terms of achieving the long term goal of Sustainable Development, the results of the research suggested that only a combination of the three approaches will deliver the paradigm change required.

6.1.2 Extracting reputational value from sustainability – closing the performance/credibility gap

In Chapter 2, I argued that sustainability issues could contribute to competitive advantage in two fundamental ways: by increasing the tangible (primarily through eco-efficiency improvements) and intangible (primarily through improved image) value of a corporation. The argument in favour of tangible value is strong but limited in its scope as a company can only be so efficient before the implementation benefits start to become less clear, the payback lengthier and the costs less justified. Chapter 2 argued that for companies to achieve sustainability they would need to go further than this. The results of my survey have suggested that CEOs expect environmental and social credibility to be important issues in sustaining a positive reputation. I therefore propose that the crucial changes needed to strive for corporate sustainability could be driven by the intangible benefits associated with corporate reputation.

In order to gain and sustain[61] a positive reputation for environmental and social performance, some MNCs will need to rethink the way they do business. As we have already seen earlier in this chapter, there are three key strategies that MNCs could follow. As 'strategy 3' is the only one that focuses on fully exploiting reputational (and therefore intangible) value, this is the strategy that this section will focus on.

The first and most important point to make is that corporate reputation/imagery will not be sustainably improved without an associated and strong performance (see Nolan, 1975). Traditional PR on its own, or the building of brand associations (cause related branding[62]) will not fool the twenty-first century stakeholder for long. Promotion must be accompanied by substance. The Shell case study in Chapter 2 has shown that it is highly dangerous for performance to come out of line with imagery – I call this lapse the 'performance/credibility gap'. In Chapter 3, I have argued that the measurement of reputation is fraught with difficulty, and, even if possible the results are not arguably of paramount use (see Proposition 6.1). The realistic measurable outcome of having a positive image is that more people will want to do business with your firm.

> Proposition 6.1
>
> Firms can manage reputation without directly measuring it. This can be achieved by combining more traditional market performance indicators with indicators of holistic corporate performance; a simple comparison will establish the extent of the gap, if any, between performance and credibility.

This is the real bottom line. Following this, I suggest that firms should redirect resources and attention from what in some cases amounts to creating unfounded imagery to the achievement of holistic performance and the associated communication of this performance to relevant stakeholders.

Measuring holistic performance

My research has suggested that companies should measure their performance in all seven reputational arenas (and not only economic performance). It is by measuring performance in all of these areas that a company could gauge its potential to gain intangible competitive advantage. If companies find that their holistic performance is good (i.e. better than their competitors) then this research suggests that they should feel free to look into ways of using this in their promotional activities[63] (see Proposition 6.2). Whether performance is good or bad, firms need to adopt a transparent communication strategy to inspire stakeholder trust and confidence.

In order to facilitate the measurement of holistic performance I suggest that it is useful to have a management framework in place that facilitates the collection of appropriate data. From the economic perspective this is all standard practice, however from the environmental and social perspective most companies will need to introduce completely new (or strongly adapted) procedures. In the case of environmental performance, environmental management systems like ISO 14001 and/or EMAS develop the appropriate competencies within organisations. From the social perspective there is less choice: in 1997 Social Accountability International launched 'SA8000' (see, www.sa8000.org), a social accountability system designed to ensure fairer and more equitable working conditions in the supply chain. In 1999, AccountAbility[64] followed this up by introducing a voluntary process standard called *AA1000*. This standard has been designed to improve overall 'corporate accountability and performance by learning through stakeholder engagement' (see, AccountAbility.org.uk for further information) and has been adopted globally by some large MNCs.

Proposition 6.2

Exemplary performance will not be enough to generate significant intangible advantage in the form of reputation; performance must be accompanied by 'effective' communication (a concept explored in the next section).

While I accept the benefits associated with the implementation of these systems, I also argue that they will have relatively little impact on overall corporate performance unless they are part of an overall 'integrated' corporate sustainability strategy. As suggested in Chapter 2, sustainability is essentially a balancing act between competing disciplines. As a result, solutions will only be reached in circumstances where an organisation has adopted an integrated approach. This is one of the primary reasons for the recent development of the *Sustainability: Integrated Guidelines for Management* (SIGMA). A joint initiative of AccountAbility, Forum for the Future, the UK Department for Trade and Industry (DTI) and the British Standards Institute (BSI), the project's main aim is to provide clear and practical advice, helping organisations to make a meaningful contribution to Sustainable Development. By showing how seemingly disparate standards can work together, the SIGMA Project effectively represents the world's only genuinely integrated approach to sustainability dilemma resolution. Based upon the findings of this research, adopting a 'SIGMA-like' approach to sustainability management would be likely to represent a significant advance in negotiating the 'virtuous responsibility circle' and attaining the objectives of 'strategy 3'.[65] Once a company has put in place a management system that facilitates the collection of appropriate data, this data will need to be analysed and communicated to interested stakeholders.

6.1.3 Effective performance communication

In Chapter 3, I have argued that the process of image formation is inherently complicated. I have also made the point that image must be grounded in substance and that communication on its own is ineffectual. On the basis of this and my results I suggest that it is a combination of the two strategies that will ultimately result in the growth of intangible value.

Stakeholders are more PR aware than they have ever been before (see Pratkanis and Aronson 1991), to the extent that the very expression or phrase 'PR' is considered in many circles to be derogatory: the voice box of scandalous, unaccountable, untrustworthy, powerful business (see, Klein 2000). But it need not be derogatory as it is ultimately a tool, a tool that is often misused but also one that is indispensable for a company wanting to extract full returns from investing in sustainability initiatives. 'Many stakeholders find companies' use of CSR as a highly visible element of ... PR efforts distasteful' (Morsing, 2003). PR clearly has a stigma attached to it, a stigma that I suggest it must remove if it is to play an effective role in the transformation of corporations. As it stands,

PR and its use has the potential to be more of a liability than an asset (see Lasn, 2000 for a well-structured argument about the development of an anti PR counter-culture).

For stakeholders to positively select a company to do business with, they must trust that company (see Golin, 2003) – not unreservedly, just more than they trust its competitors. 'The creation of trust is vital if CC[66] ... is to realise [its] full potential and play a legitimate role in 21st century society' (Lydenberg, 2003). I argue that trust can only be initiated through superior transparency and accountability. To use an analogy, unless an individual is really certain of his or her ability then he/she will not go swimming in murky water where the bottom cannot be seen, or where there is no lifeguard. PR professionals employed by companies are on the front line in the battle for trust, their position at the frontier between the company and its environment means that their actions are of paramount importance in this challenge. They are 'the water filter system in a company's swimming pool'. Without competent PR professionals, customers will choose to 'swim' elsewhere.

Having said this, accountability and transparency do not reveal the whole story. It is perfectly possible for a company to be transparent and to utilise best practice accountability – but also to be considered untrustworthy. As I argued in Chapter 3, a company must also be able to prove that their current actions form part of a long-term plan. The destination should be clear.

If one is to examine the intersection between business and society, investigating the dynamic relationship between companies and their stakeholders, it becomes evident that over time the structure is dramatically changing shape. If, as I propose, PR professionals are to manage this intersection, I suggest that they should increasingly familiarise themselves with three differing and graduated stages of engagement: 'hierarchy', 'consultancy' and finally the development of complex 'multi-level networks' (see Figure 6.2).

Hierarchy

The communication strategy of the majority of MNCs fits into this first category. Traditionally firms have concentrated on one-way flows of information, whereby the company is aware of the existence of stakeholders but, as they are not considered to be overtly influential, they are only 'communicated at' rather than being 'communicated with'. This approach is a left-over from Milton Friedman's[67] dominant, and resilient theory of the firm and the legal principle of shareholder primacy. In this model, shareholders (at the top of the hierarchy) assert their property

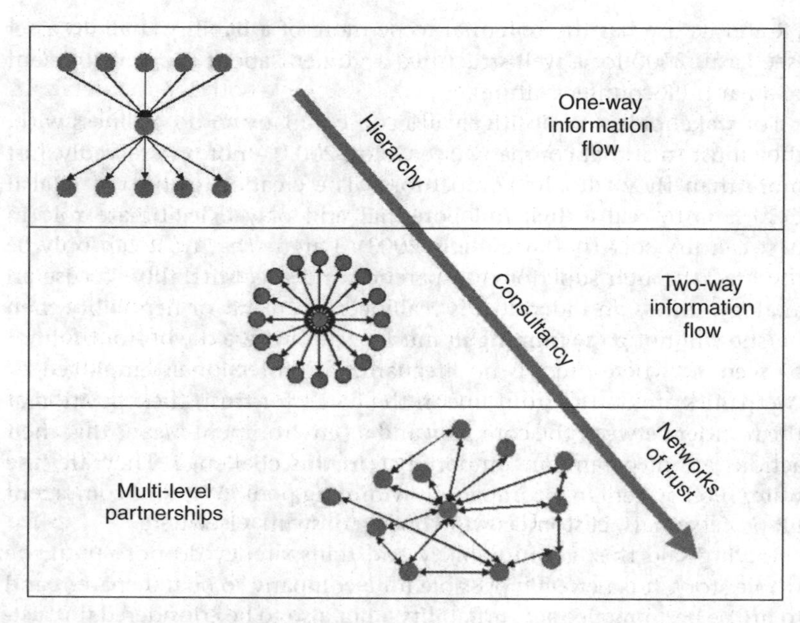

Figure 6.2 Firm/stakeholder relationships in the future.

rights and use the company simply as an instrument for wealth generation. The managers of the company concerned (schematically represented by the dot in the centre of the model – Figure 6.2) are simply agents of their owners, and as such, they are obliged to protect their interests (or what was considered to represent their interests). In the UK, while the government still acknowledges the ultimate supremacy of shareholders, in a recent review[68] they concluded that:directors should take 'a proper balanced view of the short and long term, the need to sustain effective ongoing relationships with employees, customers, suppliers and others; and the need to maintain the company's reputation and to consider the impact of its operations on the community and the environment' (Armour *et al.*, 2003).

This evolving new perspective takes us onto the second model.

Consultancy

Some other companies have noticed the benefits of applying the 'stakeholder model' to their organisation – resulting in the development of an atmosphere of two-way communication. This second model essentially replicates the relational 'hub and spoke' model introduced by

Edward. R. Freeman (Freeman, 1984). In this model stakeholders are engaged and consulted before major decisions are made. Shell and BT[69] exemplify best practice in this respect. They have both set up interactive websites – virtual forums[70] – to allow visitors to enter into dialogue on subjects that they consider of importance. Despite the innovative use of new technologies much of the theory is not new, the concept of 'stakeholder forums' find their foundations in past practices. Japanese companies for example have traditionally attributed much of their success in the 1970s, 80s and early 90s to the presence of strong stakeholder values (Plender, 1997). As Plender observes, 'Most Japanese companies are run in the interests of employees; secondarily in the interests of stakeholders such as suppliers and banks; and lastly for shareholders' (Ibid). As a result, rather than seeking consensus, Japanese firms think in terms of congruence, the implication being the development of a 'culture of dynamic reciprocity' (Hampden-Turner and Trompenaars, 1997). This innovative style of governance however is not one that has achieved universal appeal. In the US, for example, the Sarbanes-Oxley Act (rushed into place by Congress in the summer of 2002 largely as a response to the Enron affair) completely ignored stakeholder claims in favour of further entrenching accountability to shareholders (Deakin & Konzelmann, 2003). There are in fact very few examples of US companies that have adopted this style of responsive management.

While adopting a 'consultancy' style approach to stakeholder management is clearly a step in the right direction in today's interconnected world it does not go quite far enough to achieve 'strategy 3'. The 'hub and spoke' diagram (the middle illustration in Figure 6.2) describes what could be called a 'pre-Galileo[71] business environment whereby the company is seen as being in the 'centre of the universe' and stakeholders (representing societal interest) are neatly arranged in a circle around it. This diagram does little to emphasise the inclusive role of business, as a constituent part rather than as an observer within society. Businesses and the people that work within them are clearly critical and active components of our society. The diagram also suggests that each stakeholder is unconnected to the others and therefore has different or unique priorities; something that is clearly not the case in today's interconnected world. Indeed many large organisations (NGOs) have evolved to represent and champion diverse societal demands.

Networks of trust

The final model illustrated in Figure 6.2 is one that not many companies have managed to achieve. However, it does represent the rational conclusion of Freeman's original design. It involves the creation and development of not just two-way communication channels, but also partnerships,[72] where reciprocity incentivises mutual cooperation. As I have argued, today business and society are together faced by a number of complex and diversified problems,[73] partnerships offer a proven methodology to resolve some of these dilemmas (Sehested, 2003). The key difference between this model and the former being that the structure recognises that in today's world stakeholders are able to act together as partners – irrespective of whether business joins in or not. By coordinating their efforts, often in interest groups, they can more effectively achieve common aims. In the absence of the ability to play one stakeholder off against the others, I argue that it is critical for companies to have a transparent communication system. This stage reflects the fact that in the real world stakeholders are not neatly arranged in a circle around the company concerned – they can be ungrouped, grouped, close, far, big or small. Equally, and more importantly, within these networks the focus of power is not necessarily central: stakeholders can in fact display varying levels of influence and therefore the networks can be 'multi-centred'. The relationship structure between a company and its stakeholders is inherently complex, but to build trust (the real payback for a citizen company, see, Handy, 1997) companies must develop strategies to engage on these multiple levels. Once mutual trust is established the organisation itself is likely to become both more creative and more efficient (Handy, 1997). Without trust a company heavily involved with sustainability initiatives will only ever accomplish short-term, ephemeral, tangible returns and the vast potential of intangible capital may be overlooked.

The use of the word 'partnership' immediately evokes legal attention; after all, a partnership is essentially a 'legally binding cooperation between parties – both having specified and joint rights and responsibilities'.[74] In order to solve some of the complex dilemmas that face society today, the development of partnerships where rights and responsibilities are clearly defined offers a powerful way forward (see Proposition 6.3). The partnerships that I am referring to are not restrained by the law,

> Proposition 6.3
>
> Companies wanting to improve their reputation should concentrate on building networks of trust; this can be achieved through the development of transparent stakeholder partnerships.

they are quasi-legal. The hypothetical 'stick' does not threaten to bring litigation but to withdraw trust. Clearly partnerships cannot exist without mutual trust: in many ways partnerships exemplify accountability and transparency; two of the system conditions which are compulsory to the achievement of sustainability (see, Eigen, 2001). Recent stakeholder conflict[75] that companies with strong brands have witnessed is a factor of discontent (Klein, 2000). This is not only discontent with performance, but also discontent with their own ability to influence corporate behaviour. Strengthening stakeholder relationships therefore also has the side effect of reducing discontent. On the basis of this I suggest that, contrary to traditional dogma, stakeholder thinking and the development of transparent partnerships actually promotes the generation of profits – simply by paying closer attention to stakeholder demands.

The role of the PR professional

PR Week together with the PR firm Burson Marsteller recently conducted a survey asking CEOs who they would turn to to manage their corporate reputation. Sixty–Seven per cent of CEOs responded by suggesting that they would first turn to their internal PR counsel, 35 per cent suggested that they would turn to external PR professionals. On the basis of the results obtained in the research presented in this book, it would seem that if this is the case, it is not an efficient and productive situation. My research in fact suggests that PR professionals should not be relied upon to manage reputation; they should instead be challenged to create a transparent environment and manage partnership development. In a globalised world reputation will increasingly be linked to performance, perceived or otherwise. If PR professionals are seen to be managing your reputation, then conversely it could also be perceived that they are managing your performance – or, as we have seen with political parties in the UK, spinning a promotional story with little in the way of substance behind, then the truth or reality of the matter will be lost in a haze of negative publicity.

6.2 Leadership for sustainability

The credibility of leadership will have the greatest impact on maintaining the positive reputation of business in the future – so say the leaders of today's businesses. This is not a surprising conclusion.

The message that emanates from leadership shapes the culture of an organisation and facilitates reform. As argued throughout this book without strong, passionate leadership we rarely see reform. To exemplify this we need look no further than the companies that are always on the receiving end of sustainability accolades, and their leaders:

- AngloAmerican – Sir Mark Moody-Stuart
- Ben and Jerry's – Ben Cohen
- BP – Lord Browne
- DuPont – Chad Holliday
- Interface Inc. – Ray Anderson
- Patagonia – Michael W. Crooke
- STMicroelectronics – Pasquale Pistorio
- The Body Shop – Anita Roddick

I am not suggesting that any one of these organisations is sustainable (far from it in some cases!); however, each and every one of these leaders is an acknowledged and vocal convert to the cause of sustainability. The message that they send through their companies is that this is an organisational priority – and something that they see as representing an integral aspect of their holistic performance. At its root, corporate sustainability represents a cultural change for most organisations and cultural changes don't usually just spontaneously occur, they need to be stimulated from above. Without wholesale cultural change, sustainability initiatives will be unlikely to outlive the tenure of the leadership.

The message from corporate leadership has implications both within the organisation and externally with its stakeholders. For example, in a recent global survey, more than 75 per cent of respondents agreed that they have greater respect for companies when the head of the firm speaks out in favour of corporate social responsibility (Environics International, 2002). This coupled with the results of my research, confirms the existence of a strong link between the overall reputation of a company and the individual reputation of its leader.

There is something else that these kinds of leaders have in common; it is their ability to make decisions based on the long-view. Peter Drucker suggested that 'Every organization must be prepared to abandon everything it does to survive in the future' (Drucker, 1992). Although somewhat extreme, these leaders do not hesitate in echoing this view. Not only do they echo this view but many of them have laid out a road map[76] showing the organisation how they plan to survive and thrive in the future – as I suggested earlier, this represents an integral and unreplicable aspect of trust generation. Some of the companies that I have mentioned are relatively young – like the Body Shop – others, like

DuPont, are far older. Their age, however, has had no noticeable impact on their equal desire for continuance into the future.

6.2.1 Dilemma resolution; the long view versus short-termism

Clearly, a firm will have different strategic objectives depending on whether it is focused on the long term or the short term. From a distance it would seem that the focus that a company will choose to adopt will have a dramatic impact on its level of sustainability engagement.

As I have argued in Chapter 2, sustainability is about taking the long view and thinking about the long-term impacts of mankind's current activity. This way of thinking is eloquently highlighted by an old (and often quoted) Kenyan proverb which suggests that '[we] should treat the Earth well. It is not inherited from [our] parents, it is borrowed from [our] children'. Following this, Sustainable Development is a concept that affects the very survival of our society. This same idea was highlighted by Niall Fitzgerald, then CEO of Unilever, when he pronounced that 'Sustainability is here to stay, or we may not be' (in Longhurst, 2003).

Following this, and bearing in mind the need to act 'in concert' or partnership (see Chapter 2) to achieve this societal goal, the engagement of the corporate sector becomes crucial. However, if the leadership of a firm is focused on short-term profits (i.e. not focused on our collective legacy) it looks likely to be at the expense of long-term sustainability. Commentators suggest that this short-term view prevails (George, 2003) – I suggest that this is by virtue of CEOs own short 'shelf life'. According to a survey conducted by Booz Allen Hamilton between 1995 and 2001

- The turnover of the CEOs of major corporations increased by 53 per cent.
- The number of CEOs departing because of the company's poor financial performance increased by 130 percent.
- The average tenure of CEOs declined from 9.5 years to 7.3 years (Lucier *et al.*, 2002).

This study shows that CEOs are under considerable daily amount of pressure – primarily from ephemeral city investors – to report ever increasing profits, quarter by quarter. In fact, according to recent research 'today's CEO has only five earnings quarters on average to prove him or herself' (Burston-Marsteller, 2001). Lucier *et al.*, also make the point that currently 'CEOs are like professional athletes – young people with short,

> Proposition 6.4
>
> Long-term thinking is an essential pre-requisite for a company to accomplish 'strategy 3' and extract full reputational advantage from responsibility.

well-compensated careers that continue only as long as they perform at exceptional levels' (Ibid). This performance being judged purely on financial analogues and incentivised by the presence of huge financial bonuses (Plender, 1997).

By asking questions about the future, I have attempted to divorce CEOs from this pressured mindset and placed them in a world where they have to take 'the long view'. From within this long-view mindset we can observe that CEOs are aware of the strategic need to factor in the potential impact of sustainability issues on the way that they do business. In essence the results of this survey reflect what CEOs would do if they had the long-term success of their company and society foremost in their mind (see Proposition 6.4). According to the UK based Centre for Business Performance, 'the role of the board is to ensure the continued existence of the company in the long term' (The Centre for Business Performance, 2001). Obviously, and due in part to some of the cited factors, not all CEOs utilise this mindset in their day to day management and decision-making process.

As the future plays such an important part in the concept of sustainability, advocates of sustainability should investigate how to encourage long-view thinking within, and most importantly at the top of, companies.

6.2.2 Facilitating CEO future thinking

The first step, and the most difficult one, for any CEO wanting to be afforded the space to think about the future is to attempt to create a conducive external environment. I believe that this can be achieved at three levels:

1. First CEOs could lobby governments to introduce a nominal tax (something the Indian government has recently proposed) on the purchase or sale of securities. This would immediately reduce short-term trading, and force investors to seek information (other than financial) that may be a proxy of long-term corporate health.
2. Second, CEOs could go about identifying (in collaboration with other businesses in their sector), collecting and reporting on non-financial key performance indicators.

3. Third, CEOs could plausibly approach and engage institutional investors (the section of the financial community that should have a vested interest in the long term), the aim being to develop a more stable investment base.

Following the UK pensions' reform act (representing total assets of about £800bn) in 2000 (and the establishment of similar regulations in France, Australia, Germany, Sweden and Italy) many pension fund managers have a responsibility to at the very least consider environmental and social risks when making investments. Some of these fund managers are already beginning to exert pressure of their own. In a number of notable examples 'fund management' has built up a significant share in a company and then started to exercise their property rights – hijacking AGMs and bringing shareholder resolutions challenging corporate strategy. For example, in May 2003 Walden Asset Management, a socially responsible investment firm based in America, sponsored a historic shareholder resolution at Avon Products Inc. calling for the annual election of Directors. Despite being unanimously opposed by Avon's board of directors the motion was passed 80.9 per cent in favour.

If that approach fails CEOs could approach the booming SRI community; the amount of money that is invested using an SRI strategy is tripling every two years. In the US, one dollar in every eight dollars or 13 per cent of the US$16.3 trillion in investment assets, is invested in socially responsible funds. Enough funding for all but the very largest businesses.

The next stage is to create a conducive internal environment. One way to achieve this is by focusing on compensation regimes. The dominance of traditional Pay-for-Performance systems means that employees, in particular senior management, are compensated according to traditional measures of financial performance (such as Stock performance, ROS, ROA and ROE).

In more progressive organisations (those with a more inclusive definition of performance) the variable aspect of employee pay is also linked to non-financial indicators (see Proposition 6.5) balanced scorecard measures and strategic objectives, for example, customer retention, environmental performance (Alcoa provide a good example of best practice), health and safety performance (BP senior executives pay is directly related to safety performance), product quality, and so on. A progressive organisation would also extend the time line of traditional financial indicators. For example, just imagine that senior management within organisations received stock options which reflected long-term growth,

Proposition 6.5

To facilitate the growth of intangible value and to encourage 'long-term' thinking companies should base executive compensation on not just financial performance but on environmental and social as well.

not over 3 years, but 10 or 15. Sure they would still be eligible for a hefty pay cheque, commensurate with their position, but, the rest was payable in time-secured stocks. Let's say 10 per cent redeemable on retirement, 35 per cent in 5 years, 40 per cent in 10 years, and 15 per cent held in trust for their children.

I think that overnight we would have a different attitude in the board room. An effective manager could potentially not only make money in the short term but also secure an income stream for his/her family in the future.

Despite all this, taking the long view is not the only pre-requisite for increasing overall corporate engagement in sustainability. The three response strategies outlined earlier make it clear that sustainability engagement also brings tangible short-term benefits. Eco-efficiency[77] is a concept that immediately comes to mind, the practice of reducing resource usage as a factor of each product made. However, whilst short-term savings can be dramatic (see DeSimone and Popoff, 1997) this 'end of pipe[78] attitude and short-termism as a mindset, on its own, will do nothing to increase a company's intangible value – certainly not to the extent that it can be used as competitive advantage. As a society (in the prosperous North) we consume far too much (Ryan, 2002), short-term efficiency increases and the like will do little or nothing to quell this engrained cultural appetite. The problem associated with short-termism is not lack of opportunity, but presence of risk. If corporate leadership were forced (by circumstances) to persist in taking the short-view, they would not be able to avoid the risk of being seen to be actively avoiding societal expectations. The only real way to avoid this risk is to adopt 'strategy 3' and engage in sustainability with an eye to the future.

The 'adversary' of widespread corporate sustainability engagement is not however wholly the short view. This certainly does not help but the adversary really lays in a widespread misunderstanding/misinterpretation of the key issues and their associated risk/opportunity profile. The sooner companies appreciate the benefits of adopting an integrated mindset – balancing short and long views – the sooner they can lower their exposure to risk and start to reap the benefits of positive corporate imagery.

6.3 Partnerships for sustainability

A partner, in the business context, is defined by the *Oxford English Dictionary* as being someone who is associated with someone else in order to 'share risks and profits'. This seems relatively clear, however here I am not referring to business partners, I am referring specifically to non-traditional partnerships whereby the common goal is some form of societal or environmental improvement. The partners of business in projects of this nature tend to fit into the following categories:

- NGOs and special interest groups (e.g. Amnesty International, Greenpeace, Christian Aid).
- Governmental agencies (local, national and international).
- Other businesses (individual businesses or business interest groups).
- Educational establishments (e.g. universities, schools and colleges).
- Individuals (e.g. famous or wealthy individuals, like U2's Bono, who have a particular or specific interest).

Transparency and accountability

Transparency and accountability have become the mantra of many contemporary businesses. This behavioural change has in part been driven by several of the groupings listed earlier. Unfortunately, as many of these groupings have grown in size and influence, their transparency and accountability has failed to keep pace. This applies particularly to NGOs, the majority of whom are almost completely opaque, and only marginally unaccountable. These organisations find themselves in the position where they are themselves not 'practicing what they preach'. For example, how many NGOs report on their financial performance? The answer is a handful, even fewer report in a formal recognised way on their environmental and social performance. How many NGOs have a formalised governance code? Again the answer is very few.

Having singled out NGOs it is worth pointing out that government agencies and educational establishments are not entirely exempt from blame. For example, it is increasingly difficult to establish the funding/ income streams for university departments and research projects. If it is possible to view the funding stream, it is even more difficult to understand how the decision to partner was made. Universities often seem to fail to understand that, although partnership represents an important funding stream, it also represents endorsement. Not actual endorsement, but perceived, and as we have seen above, in today's globalised world perceptions are often more important than reality. In recent years scepticism has resided firmly in the hands of NGOs, today businesses often look towards NGOs and other potential partners with a degree of suspicion. Smart business is, quite justifiably, increasingly unwilling to engage, let alone to partner with, organisations that do not at the very least mirror their own efforts at transparency.

6.3.1 Avoiding partnership pitfalls

As we have already seen, corporate reputation and brand value are fragile, sensitive, yet highly valuable resources; intangible resources that businesses spend vast sums of money to bolster. Really no wonder, when you consider that very few firms could continue to trade successfully without their positive imagery.

It is for this reason that I propose that companies need to be far more careful with the way that they currently partner with the organisations listed earlier. Currently, and in part due to the discourse adopted at RIO + 10, businesses are frantically partnering, or engaging with the organisations that they once fought. The underlying theory being this: We are not trusted, therefore let's partner with someone else who has a higher capital stock of trust – that way we will be more trusted by association. There are many very clear examples of this practice, however you will not find them listed here in this paper, primarily because businesses are understandably nervous about commentators putting pen to paper. They consider tangible threats to their reputation very seriously indeed, even if they have arguably already happened.

However, this is not the whole story, by partnering with other organisations, companies are, subconsciously, drawing a link between the values and brand message of the partner, with their own. It must be remembered that in the main NGOs are founded on a set of core values, a set of values that are immovable, a set of values upon which their own licence to operate is founded. In the short term, from the trust perspective, this 'sharing of values' may look like a very good idea, perhaps you both share a spatial interest in HIV/AIDS in sub-Saharan Africa, inner city poverty, or birdlife in south western England. But by partnering you are also, perhaps unwittingly, aligning yourself with past and future activities of that partner. Not only are you doing that, you are also potentially creating inherent contradictions in your brand message. For example, on the one hand you may be telling your consumers to buy more of your product, however, on the other hand you are partnering with an organisation whose long-term goal is to reduce consumerism – thereby reducing your profit margin.

For any partnership to be instigated it needs to be rooted in some form of common goal or vision. This does not mean that both organisations goals and visions need to be completely aligned, but there needs to be some clear, common link to justify the engagement. In many cases this decision making process appears to have been overlooked; the desire to 'partner', and the perceived individual benefits, have outweighed the need to explore commonalities. Unfortunately for the partners, observant stakeholders can fairly easily determine, or assume individual benefits from the exterior. Limited liability legislation means that the average commercial business is constrained by the need to be focused on financial returns, and an NGO is likely to be heavily focused on some specific form of non-financial progress. There is an inherent conflict between the purest forms of these two ideologies. Government departments have highly politicised goals and other businesses may well have your customers in their sights.

Core mutual objectives aside, from the reputational perspective for a partnership to be successful it must pass the external plausibility test. Stakeholders are almost always suspicious of business and its reasoning. With this as a backdrop businesses should ask themselves what an independent observer would make of each potential link-up. In many cases this process will highlight and possibly pre-empt reputational problems. Taken on face value a partnership with a high profile charity may seem like a good idea, on the other hand (depending on the sector) consumers may find this to be in contradiction with corporate behaviour, both past and present. If this is found to be the case then for the partnership to be reputationally successful the company must ensure that the partnership is fully transparent, is accompanied by stakeholder dialogue, and has observable and measurable outcomes. Not only this, the company must make a public commitment to changing its behaviour in the areas of inherent partner conflict. Without this commitment stakeholders will, perhaps rightly, assume that the company is partnering for reasons of self-interest – the anti-thesis of many peoples definition of corporate responsibility.

Five rules for partnership

Twenty-first century business is powerful, but despite the much publicised rhetoric of the anti-globalisation lobby, it cannot strive towards sustainability without taking other societal actors with it. I believe that the responsibility, if indeed we can find a concrete one, rests firmly in the sphere of individuals. Business is only one emanation of society that contains individuals. Sustainability is everybody's responsibility.

Business must play its role as a 'citizen' within society – to do this effectively it must partner. Clearly there are risks associated with this practice however I argue that the risks are outweighed by the benefits if business observes the following five rules:

1. Always conduct 'stakeholder consultation' prior to partnering to gauge external perception,
2. Carefully examine partner 'transparency' and motives,
3. Ensure that you have a set of 'common values' and mutual partnership 'objectives',
4. From the outset clearly state partnership 'timeline' and limits of behaviour,
5. 'Report' on the nature and financial value of the partnership externally.

No approach is risk free, but by following these pointers business can avoid most pitfalls.

6.4 The SME perspective

This research has focused on large MNCs – in fact, more specifically, the largest 500 companies in the world. However, the research does also have fundamental implications for other smaller enterprises.

As big business struggles to enhance or sustain its intangible value, this research has shown that it will need to improve its performance in seven key areas (the 'seven elements of reputation'). As argued in Chapter 2 – this is a task that big business cannot undertake alone. The reasoning? Because big business does not act alone – big business is only a link in a long and extensive supply chain (both upstream and downstream). To make real performance improvements, all parties concerned will need to be engaged into action. This is not a new phenomenon; many MNCs currently impose supply chain demands based upon their own performance obligations, for example, among other things *ISO 14001*[79] (environmental management standard) certification. In 1998, for example, General Motors Corp. (GM) announced their intention to certify all their facilities to *ISO 14001*. Together with this announcement, they advised their top 600 vehicle parts suppliers that they required them to become certified to an Environmental Management

> Proposition 6.6
>
> In the near future good environmental and social performance will be of critical, tangible importance to SMEs looking to partner with multinational businesses.

System equivalent to *ISO14001* by the end of 2002. 'This requirement applies to all supplier facilities that provide parts to *GM* and that have a significant environmental impact and to suppliers whose current or future contracts extend, or might extend, beyond 2002.'[80] If GM had not applied such pressure on its supply chain, its own performance and reputation could have been put in jeopardy. In another prime example, both Nike and The Gap have experienced direct damage to their intangible value due to the poor performance of their suppliers – in these cases poor labour conditions and illegal child labour as exposed by the media and NGOs are the cited problems (Kenyon, 2000). In a number of cases – GM being an example – the MNC concerned would be so keen to improve holistic performance that it will help (read: pay for) SMEs to adapt/improve their operating procedures and so on (see Proposition 6.6).

In summary the decisions that CEOs of today's MNCs are making with respect to corporate sustainability look set to very quickly filter down the supply chain, impacting even the smallest companies. Following this, SMEs are also presented with three strategic options – exactly the same strategic options that face MNCs (see Figure 6.1). There is however one crucial difference: MNCs are primarily looking to improve/retain their intangible value – for SMEs (which do not necessarily benefit from strong, highly visible, global brands) sustainability could develop as being altogether more tangible; as a prerequisite to building lucrative MNC partnerships, it could easily become a question of survival. In terms of the 'three drivers of corporate sustainability' model outlined in Chapter 2 it is possible to observe that for SMEs the 'stick' is likely to become the most powerful change agent.

6.5 Global variation

Not surprisingly, the survey has highlighted some very clear and notable regional differences of opinion. For example, companies based in North America assign a lower level of importance to EC and SC than companies based in Europe or elsewhere. The North America versus Europe contrast is not astonishing; however, the obvious engagement of companies based elsewhere did come as a surprise. The average North

American CEOs' opinion on the future importance of sustainability issues lags behind the rest of the industrialised world. While this is to an extent, depressing, I believe that this probably reveals more about the current political, and resulting regulatory climate in North America than personal aspirations and ideology. Equally it takes away from some of the cutting edge corporate sustainability initiatives that are currently taking place in US companies – many of whom are outside the Global Fortune 500, but may well be in it in five or ten years time!

Although some of these differences are statistically significant, it is the similarity in response which I believe should merit greater attention. In each individual region, sustainability issues (EC, SC and FC) were never considered to be of lower than medium importance. This (Proposition 6.7) is supported by the key finding of a recent PricewaterhouseCoopers survey. They also found that CEOs from the EU and US displayed similar differences in attitude on social and environmental issues. The Report concluded that 'Environmental and Social Performance [is considered to be] a Priority for Europeans; [and] an Opportunity for Americans' (PricewaterhouseCoopers, 2003). This result is disputable, I would argue that US firms are more focused on risk and European firms are more focused on opportunity, but still, disputes and differences aside, the salient point is that both approaches display a significant level of interest and concern. Following the results of my survey the question is no longer whether EC and SC are important, but rather, what can be done to enhance them? As we discovered in Chapter 2, for many large MNCs preparing for this future positioning will represent a significant mindset, attitudinal and strategic change.

In retrospect, the differences observed between regions are certainly worthy of greater attention and scrutiny. For example, using the current regional breakdown, the United Kingdom's responses are considered together with the rest of continental Europe. It would be interesting to see whether the US response was mirrored in the UK (showing a common Anglo-Saxon approach) or whether we align more closely with continental Europe. Unfortunately with my existing confidentiality clause this would not have been possible. However, if the sample size

> Proposition 6.7
>
> Wherever a company is based, large MNCs should expect EC and SC to be of at least medium significance to the preservation of a positive corporate reputation.

were larger, I could have afforded to relax the clause and directly compare responses from individual countries.

6.6 The role of the financial community

In Chapter 2 the role of the financial community in achieving corporate sustainability was briefly touched upon. It was suggested that financial institutions appear to be more engaged in the corporate sustainability field than their peers. The results of hypothesis 5.2 showed that this was not the case, although financiers did consider social and environmental credibility to be at least as significant (at 5 per cent) to the preservation of a positive corporate reputation as their peers. This conclusion does not square with much of the research conducted in the EU. Jeucken, for example, found that 'the banking sector has responded far more slowly than other sectors to the new challenges that sustainability presents', and went on to suggest that 'a large group of banks still do not see the role they can play and maybe should play towards a sustainable development' (Jeucken, 2001). Perhaps Jeucken is correct and financial institutions are still relatively un-engaged in sustainability issues; however, the results of this survey suggest that in the near future they are expecting to have to make significant changes to the way that they operate. Change is certainly on the horizon.

If, as the survey suggests, financiers are starting to become concerned about their own EC and SC it would seem obvious that they are also planning to use these as criteria for making/planning their investments. This likelihood is evidenced most clearly in the report 'Who Cares Wins: Connecting Financial Markets to a Changing World', issued in 2004 at the United Nations Global Compact's Leaders Summit. The report details recommendations by the financial industry to better integrate environmental, social and governance issues into investment analysis, asset management and securities brokerage. The concluding statement is signed by a long list of traditional mainstream investors including: BNP Paribas, Credit Suisse Group, Deutsche Bank, Goldman Sachs, Morgan Stanley, RCM and UBS. The report clearly states that these investors believe that there is a clear link between management of environmental, social and corporate governance (ESG) factors and overall corporate performance. By taking account of corporate performance in these areas they believe that they can both improve market stability and reduce investment risk.

This research, taken together with the results of my survey should therefore serve as a warning for sustainability laggards – who are not only going to miss out on the significant 'ethical' investment market (which is predicted to grow – see Chapter 2) but who may also find themselves being left on the sidelines during conventional investment deals.

6.7 List of key propositions

Proposition 5.1: In the near future EC and SC are predicted to play an important role in maintaining a positive corporate reputation.

Proposition 5.2: In the near future EC and SC will be of importance to the preservation of a positive corporate reputation, not individually but as part of a broad spectrum of interrelated issues (see the other elements of reputation).

Proposition 5.3: Public perception of leadership style will be the single most important factor influencing overall corporate reputation in the future.

Proposition 6.1: Firms can manage reputation without directly measuring it. This can be achieved by combining more traditional market performance indicators with indicators of holistic corporate performance; a simple comparison will establish the extent of the gap, if any, between performance and credibility.

Proposition 6.2: Exemplary performance will not be enough to generate significant intangible advantage in the form of reputation; performance must be accompanied by 'effective' communication.

Proposition 6.3: Companies wanting to improve their reputation should concentrate on building networks of trust; this can be achieved through the development of transparent stakeholder partnerships.

Proposition 6.4: Long-term thinking is an essential pre-requisite for a company to accomplish 'strategy three' and extract full reputational advantage from responsibility.

Proposition 6.5: To facilitate the growth of intangible value and to encourage 'long-term' thinking companies should base executive compensation on not just financial performance but also environmental and social.

Proposition 6.6: In the near future good environmental and social performance will be of critical, tangible importance to SMEs looking to partner with multinational businesses.

Proposition 6.7: Wherever a company is based, large MNCs should expect EC and SC to be of at least medium significance to the preservation of a positive corporate reputation.

6.8 The seven transitions

The conclusions of this book have been presented in two separate ways. First, I have made ten key propositions. Second, I have highlighted a number of transitions inherent in the dynamic relationship between today's large MNCs and society (argued on the basis of a combination of the results of my survey with the literature and practice reviews in Chapters 2 and 3). I argue that the successful management of these seven transitions is essential to the mitigation of risk and extraction of reputational value from sustainability. This conclusion distils each of these directional changes and in doing so, presents a unique and revealing agenda for business and academia to further investigate/attempt to resolve.

6.8.1 Transition 1: From tangible to intangible

Sustainability as a concept appears to be finally stealing away from the drawing board. The responses of Global business leaders make it very clear that the underlying conceptual issues are here to stay and they expect them to have a significant impact on the reputation of their businesses. As our economy changes shape from being primarily based on tangible growth to being chiefly driven by the growth of intangibles, the preservation of positive reputation becomes ever more important both to corporate survival and to the development of competitive advantage. In the short term, sustainability offers companies a clear opportunity to make tangible cost savings and improve overall management style. However, my research has shown that, in the long term, sustainability offers businesses a massive opportunity to define themselves from their competitors and unearth theoretically inexhaustible stocks of intangible capital.

6.8.2 Transition 2: From short to long

The responses to this survey suggest that the CEOs of the world's largest companies are very aware of the long-term business case for sustainability. The question then arises as to why they are not implementing it? I have argued that the explanation for this is that they are not given the freedom to think in a long-term mindset. I have proposed that long-term thinking can be encouraged in several key ways: by making changes to the way that senior executives are compensated; by engaging with the financial community; by increasing stakeholder involvement in the decision-making process (partnership development); and/or, by employing the services of a strong, visionary figurehead.

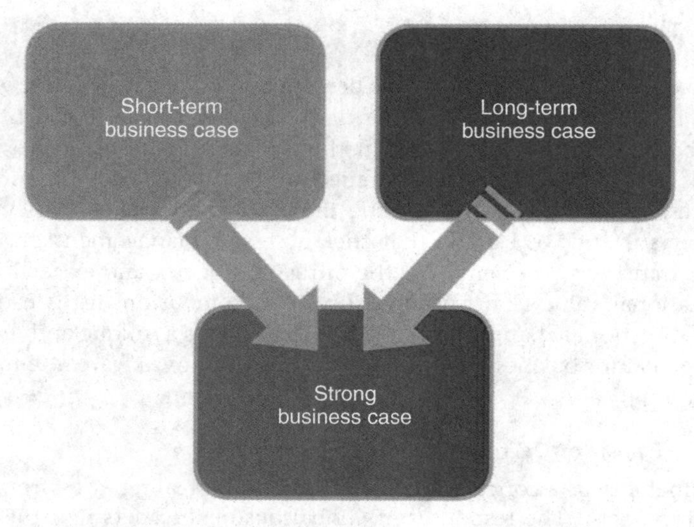

Figure 6.3 Constructing a strong business case on two levels.

Having said this, I concede that business must also act on, and be aware of, the short-term case for change. I have proposed that maximum 'buy-in' can be achieved by constructing a business case on two distinct levels as shown in Figure 6.3.

Ultimately, I suggest that if corporate leadership is able to synthesise these two distinct levels of thinking (both long and short) the business case for sustainability is strong.

6.8.3 Transition 3: From linear to cyclical

I have proposed that, to date, linear thinking has hampered the extraction of reputational value from sustainability. In the past when businesses have made improvements in their environmental or social performance they have immediately employed the assistance of their PR departments to extract value, or competitive advantage. This process has frequently led to conflict and misunderstanding between business and society. I have suggested that this misalignment occurs because value and advantage are not the endgame, but by-products of a cyclical system. As with any by-product, it is unlikely to be fully available until the manufacturing process itself has been completed (the 'Virtuous responsibility circle' – see Figure 2.8). Assuming that a manufacturing process is stopped the moment that a by-product is produced (current practice), the by-product would then become the 'product'. Stakeholders would then be free to assume that the sustainability engagement was instigated solely because of the reputational value that it would bring. I have argued that it is far better to get on with the processes, repeating/refining them and constructing networks of trust; after all, more completed revolutions of the circle would mean more by-product (enhanced reputation) produced.

6.8.4 Transition 4: From image to reality

In order to grow and sustain intangible value in 'the global goldfish bowl', I have proposed that business will need to ensure that its image meets reality, irrespective of whether real performance is negative or positive. In an environment whereby stakeholders have the ability to observe both the presented image and a multitude of other images, I suggest that it is important to retain credibility and trust. In order to bridge a gap of this nature, I have argued that a company must communicate not only holistic performance but also, more importantly, strategic direction. Although it is an extreme example, business can learn from international diplomacy: for example, during the recent second Gulf war, Iraqi information minister Muhammed Saeed al-Sahaf became the subject of Western ridicule for allowing the gap between image and reality to become insurmountable. His frequent press statements were completely false; and the public was aware of this because they could watch something which approximated to reality on their own televisions.

6.8.5 Transition 5: From suspicion to trust

The recently developed and now powerful anti-globalisation lobby has succeeded in instigating a great deal of suspicion and public distrust in business. Their arguments are in many cases clear and poignant. I have proposed that this suspicion is first, a factor of corporate use of false and/or dubious imagery, and second, the result of perceived inequitable power relations between business and society.

By moving from image to reality business has the potential to move from suspicion to trust. This move is of fundamental importance, because, as I have suggested earlier, this trust can represent the real return on responsibility. I have shown that without trust between company and stakeholder, the relationship is invariably weak and potentially transient. In order to resolve the power relations debate, I have suggested that businesses should first ask the right questions displaying a willingness to face up to the big issues of the day[81] and, second, not only listen to stakeholders but also be seen to act on the results. For the stakeholder/partnership model to work, stakeholders need to feel that they can have a real influence on outcomes.

6.8.6 Transition 6: From local to global

I have argued that CSR and/or CC are processes that have been practised by some companies for years. Prominent historical examples of best practice include Cadbury's, Lever Brothers, Toyota, and FIAT.[82] Companies felt that they had a responsibility to their local community and consequentially invested heavily in it; CSR has historically been local. Following the onset and maturing of globalisation, the sphere within which companies operate has grown wider. The world has become what is often called a 'global village'. Despite these colossal changes, a number of prominent companies could be accused of practising CSR solely in their own back-yards, taking little or no account of their activities or impact in the less developed world. MNCs are by definition global, their huge profits are derived on a global scale, therefore their responsibilities should also be global. Following this research, I propose that protagonists of the ideology of responsibility cease talking about CSR and CC as if they were new concepts and redesign them to fit this new socio- political landscape. This does not require a great deal of thought – indeed much of the leg-work has already been done: the concept of 'corporate sustainability' was designed explicitly to meet these new requirements.

6.8.7 Transition 7: From pushed to accompanied

Throughout this book I have proposed that the role of visionary leadership in the quest for corporate sustainability, while not essential, is clearly one of the most powerful agents for change. It is partially through leadership that strategic direction is communicated – one of the more important aspects of trust building. I have suggested that without a clear understanding of strategic direction, stakeholders are more likely to assume that a company is acting purely on the grounds of self-interest. I have shown that in a number of prominent cases behavioural changes towards more responsible behaviour have been driven by disaster. From the reputational perspective it is infinitely better to be seen to pre-emptively change course, preferably after extensive stakeholder consultation. If a company frequently acts in concert (while maintaining awareness of the 'partnership pitfalls' highlighted earlier in this chapter) with its stakeholders, it will be far more difficult for those same stakeholders to take unilateral action against the company's strategic direction.

6.9 Implications for further research

Corporate sustainability, the triple bottom line, reputation, CSR, and other such are without a doubt the buzz words of business today; there can be few other subjects in the business world that are discussed with greater frequency. On a global scale almost every think-tank, consultancy, business publication or academic institution is frantically trying to prove its experience and competency in the field. In the main, multinational business is running scared, consultancies are seeing dollar signs, and academia is setting up courses and research groups (even, in one case, a subject specific MBA) faster than they can be counted.

Many of these groups are engaged in outlining what they call the 'business case' for change. Following the findings of this research, it would seem that future investigations need no longer look at whether it is important for companies to improve their environmental and social credibility (the CEOs of the Global Fortune 500 are already convinced) but to establish how they should go about doing this, and then in turn how they should publicise this performance among their stakeholders. In doing so, companies will ultimately be able to close up the virtuous cycle of responsibility (see Figure 2.8) extracting a tangible return on responsibility. It does not seem to be particularly time-efficient for future researchers to be further describing and recounting the drivers for change, after all most of these drivers will be quite unique to each particular sector and even to individual businesses. Companies and their stakeholders want to know not 'why', but 'how' to respond to the challenge that sustainable development presents. CEOs and the businesses that they represent are now likely to want to focus on the nuts and bolts of implementation. As the CSR and corporate sustainability debate emerges from its 'primeval ooze' state it seems likely that the PR bubble which currently surrounds it is likely to burst, leaving us with nothing but the reality. Interesting business case, great report – but how are you going to do it all, and when?

Following on from this, areas that would benefit from enhanced research include:

- Integrated sustainability management systems and guidelines,
- The development of sector specific key sustainability indicators,
- User targeted – integrated performance reporting,

- Stakeholder engagement techniques,
- Means of senior executive compensation.

In the meantime, I very much hope that the results of this research have contributed to a better understanding of the critical role of reputation and imagery in the quest for corporate sustainability.

Appendices

Appendix 1: The survey

Front Page

CAMBRIDGE GLOBAL RESEARCH PROGRAMME: THE FUTURE OF CORPORATE REPUTATIONS

UNIVERSITY OF CAMBRIDGE
Judge Institute of Management
cambridge's business school

This survey forms part of a research programme at the University of Cambridge in the UK. Through dialogue with global leaders it aims to establish how corporate reputations will be constructed and sustained in the future.

Arlo. K. O. Brady,
Cambridge, England, June, 2002

INSTRUCTIONS

1: Read Individual Scenario[1] (there are three in total)
2: Visualise the resulting impacts on the reputation of your company
3: Tick the Appropriate Boxes
4: Return the Survey.

- An explanation of the 7 elements of reputation can be found on the enclosed bookmark
- For more detailed instructions, see back of cover letter.

TROUBLESHOOTING IS AVAILABLE ONLINE AT WWW.ARLOBRADY.COM

SCENARIO ONE: FORTRESS WORLD

Fortress World is a vision based not only on the failure of market led growth to redress social wrongs and prevent environmental disasters but also on the belief that unconstrained markets will exacerbate these problems and that large portions of humanity will be left out of the prosperity that markets bring. These failures eventually destroy the resources and the social framework on which markets and economic growth depend. Economic stagnation spreads as more resources are diverted to maintain security and stability, as does economic fragmentation where conflict dominates or the social order breaks down. The scenario describes a future in which enclaves of wealth and prosperity coexist with widening misery and growing desperation, a future of inequality, violence, conflict and instability[2].

Given the scenario 'Fortress World' please rate the seven elements of reputation for their ***probable*** *significance to the preservation of a positive corporate reputation.*

Elements of Reputation	SIGNIFICANCE (Tick one box on each line)			
	High	Med	Low	None
Knowledge & Skills				
Emotional Connections				
Leadership, Vision & Desire				
Quality				
Financial Credibility				
Social Credibility				
Environmental Credibility				

PLEASE TURN OVER……

[1] Hammond, A. (1998). Which World? Scenarios for the 21st Century. London, Earthscan Publications Ltd

[2] International Centre for Integrative Studies. (2000). Environmental Issues Series No 17, Cloudy Crystal Balls: 58-61

ID Number (for mailing purposes only). Confidentiality is guaranteed:

Back Page

SCENARIO TWO: MARKET WORLD

This scenario describes a future based on the belief that market forces and new technology will lead to rising prosperity and will offer humanity a bright future, a future in which markets rule and global corporations dominate. Economic reform and technological innovation fuel rapid economic growth. Developing regions are integrated into the global economy, creating a powerful global market, and bringing modern techniques and products to virtually all countries. The result is widespread prosperity, peace and stability[2].

Given the scenario 'Market World' please rate the seven elements of reputation for their ***probable*** *significance to the preservation of a positive corporate reputation.*

Elements of Reputation	SIGNIFICANCE (Tick one box on each line)			
	High	Med	Low	None
Knowledge & Skills				
Emotional Connections				
Leadership, Vision & Desire				
Quality				
Financial Credibility				
Social Credibility				
Environmental Credibility				

SCENARIO THREE: TRANSFORMED WORLD

In this scenario fundamental social and political change, and perhaps even changed values and cultural norms, give rise to enlightened policies and voluntary actions that direct or supplement market forces. Transformed World envisions a society in which power is more widely shared and in which new social coalitions work from the grassroots up to shape what institutions and governments do. Democratic forms of government become almost universal and a spiritual revival triggers a surge in private philanthropy. Although markets become effective tools for economic progress, they do not substitute for deliberate social choices; economic competition exists but does not outweigh the larger needs for cooperation and solidarity among the world's peoples and for the fulfilment of basic human needs[2].

Given the scenario 'Transformed World' please rate the seven elements of reputation for their ***probable*** *significance to the preservation of a positive corporate*

Elements of Reputation	SIGNIFICANCE (Tick one box on each line)			
	High	Med	Low	None
Knowledge & Skills				
Emotional Connections				
Leadership, Vision & Desire				
Quality				
Financial Credibility				
Social Credibility				
Environmental Credibility				

TO REQUEST A COPY OF THE FREE SUMMARY REPORT PLEASE TICK BOX ☐

THANKS FOR YOUR TIME!

PLEASE RETURN THE COMPLETED SURVEY TO ME IN THE PRE-PAID ENVELOPE ENCLOSED.

COMMENTS:

CONTACT ME:

Ado. K. O. Brady,
The Judge Institute of Management,
Cambridge University,
Trumpington Street,
Cambridge,
CB2 1AG, UK

T: +44 (0) 7712 651091
F: +44 (0) 1223 339701
E: a.brady@jims.cam.ac.uk
W: www.arobrady.com

Appendix 2: The year 2001 Global Fortune 500

The following is a full list of all the companies whose CEO was asked to participate in the survey. The companies listed were all part of the year 2001 Global Fortune 500 and as such, at the time, they were the world's largest 500 companies (by revenue): The list itself is © 2001 Time Inc.

The CEOs of all of the companies on this list received a copy of my survey. It is important to note that presence on this list does not indicate a positive or negative response.

Company name	Industry	Country
ABB	Electronics, Electrical Equipment	Switzerland
Abbey National	Banks – commercial and savings	Britain
Abbott Laboratories	Pharmaceuticals	USA
ABN AMRO Holding	Banks – commercial and savings	Netherlands
Adecco	Diversified outsourcing services	Switzerland
Aegon	Insurance – life, health (stock)	Netherlands
Aetna	Health care	USA
Agricultural Bank of China	Banks – commercial and savings	China
Air France Group	Airlines	France
Akzo Nobel	Chemicals	Netherlands
Albertson's	Food and drug stores	USA
Alcatel	Telecommunications	France
Alcoa	Metals	USA
All Nippon Airways	Airlines	Japan
Allianz	Insurance – P & C (stock)	Germany
Allstate	Insurance – P & C (stock)	USA
Almanij	Banks – commercial and savings	Belgium
Alstom	Industrial and farm equipment	France
Amerada Hess	Petroleum refining	USA
American Electric Power	Utilities – gas and electric	USA
American Express	Diversified financials	USA
American General	Insurance – life, health (stock)	USA
American Home Products	Pharmaceuticals	USA
American International Group	Insurance – P & C (stock)	USA
AmerisourceBergen Corporation	Wholesalers: health care	USA
AMP	Insurance – life, health (stock)	Australia
AMR	Airlines	USA
Anglo American	Mining, crude-oil production	Britain
Anheuser-Busch	Beverages	USA

Continued

Appendix 2 Continued

Company name	Industry	Country
Arbed	Metals	Luxembourg
Archer Daniels Midland	Food production	USA
Arrow Electronics	Wholesalers – electronics and office equipment	USA
Asahi Glass	Building materials, glass	Japan
Asahi Kasei	Chemicals	Japan
Asahi Mutual Life Insurance	Insurance – life, health (mutual)	Japan
Assicurazioni Generali	Insurance – life, health (stock)	Italy
Astrazeneca	Pharmaceuticals	Britain
AT&T	Telecommunications	USA
AutoNation	Specialty retailers	USA
Aventis	Pharmaceuticals	France
AXA	Insurance – life, health (stock)	France
BAE Systems	Aerospace and defense	Britain
Banco Bilbao Vizcaya Argentaria	Banks – commercial and savings	Spain
Banco Bradesco	Banks – commercial and savings	Brazil
Banco Do Brasil	Banks – commercial and savings	Brazil
Bank of America Corp.	Banks – commercial and savings	USA
Bank of China	Banks – commercial and savings	China
Bank of Montreal	Banks – commercial and savings	Canada
Bank of Nova Scotia	Banks – commercial and savings	Canada
Bank of Scotland	Banks – commercial and savings	Britain
Bank of Tokyo-Mitsubishi	Banks – commercial and savings	Japan
Bank One Corp.	Banks – commercial and savings	USA
Barclays	Banks – commercial and savings	Britain
Basf	Chemicals	Germany
Bayer	Chemicals	Germany
Bayerische Landesbank	Banks – commercial and savings	Germany
BCE	Telecommunications	Canada
BellSouth	Telecommunications	USA
Bergen Brunswig	Wholesalers: health care	USA
Berkshire Hathaway	Insurance – P & C (stock)	USA
Bertelsmann	Publishing, printing	Germany
Best Buy	Specialty retailers	USA
BHP	Mining, crude-oil production	Australia
BMW	Motor vehicles and parts	Germany
BNP Paribas	Banks – commercial and savings	France
Boeing	Aerospace and defense	USA
Bouygues	Engineering, construction	France
BP	Petroleum refining	Britain
Bridgestone	Rubber and plastic products	Japan
Bristol-Myers Squibb	Pharmaceuticals	USA
British Airways	Airlines	Britain

Continued

Appendix 2 Continued

Company name	Industry	Country
British American Tobacco	Tobacco	Britain
BT	Telecommunications	Britain
Cable & Wireless	Telecommunications	Britain
Canadian Imperial Bank of Commerce	Banks – commercial and savings	Canada
Canadian Pacific	Energy	Canada
Canon	Computers, office equipment	Japan
Cardinal Health	Wholesalers – health care	USA
Carrefour	Food and drug stores	France
Carso Global Telecom	Telecommunications	Mexico
Caterpillar	Industrial and farm equipment	USA
Central Japan Railway	Railroads	Japan
Centrica	Utilities – gas and electric	Britain
Cepsa	Petroleum refining	Spain
Cgnu	Insurance – life, health (stock)	Britain
Chevron	Petroleum refining	USA
China Construction Bank	Banks – commercial and savings	China
China Mobile Communications	Telecommunications	China
China National Petroleum	Energy	China
China Telecommunications	Telecommunications	China
Christian Dior	Miscellaneous	France
Chubu Electric Power	Utilities – gas and electric	Japan
Cigna	Health care	USA
Circuit City Stores	Specialty retailers	USA
Cisco Systems	Network and other communications equipment	USA
Citigroup	Diversified financials	USA
CNP Assurances	Insurance – life, health (stock)	France
Coca-Cola	Beverages	USA
Coca-Cola Enterprises	Beverages	USA
Cofco	Trading	China
Coles Myer	Food and drug stores	Australia
Commerzbank	Banks – commercial and savings	Germany
Compaq Computer	Computers, office equipment	USA
Computer Sciences	Computer services and software	USA
ConAgra	Food consumer products	USA
Conoco	Petroleum refining	USA
Consignia	Mail, package, freight delivery	Britain
Corus Group	Metals	Britain
Cosmo Oil	Petroleum refining	Japan
Costco Wholesale	Specialty retailers	USA

Continued

Appendix 2 Continued

Company name	Industry	Country
Crédit Agricole	Banks – commercial and savings	France
Credit Lyonnais	Banks – commercial and savings	France
Credit Suisse	Banks – commercial and savings	Switzerland
CVS	Food and drug stores	USA
Dai Nippon Printing	Publishing, printing	Japan
Daido Life Insurance	Insurance – life, health (mutual)	Japan
Daiei	General merchandisers	Japan
Dai-ichi Mutual Life Insurance	Insurance – life, health (mutual)	Japan
Daimler Chrysler	Motor vehicles and parts	Germany
Dana	Motor vehicles and parts	USA
Deere	Industrial and farm equipment	USA
Delhaize 'Le Lion'	Food and drug stores	Belgium
Dell Computer	Computers, office equipment	USA
Delphi Automotive	Motor vehicles and parts	USA
Delta Air Lines	Airlines	USA
Denso	Motor vehicles and parts	Japan
Dentsu	zMiscellaneous	Japan
Deutsche Bahn	Railroads	Germany
Deutsche Bank	Banks – commercial and savings	Germany
Deutsche Post	Mail, package, freight delivery	Germany
Deutsche Telekom	Telecommunications	Germany
Dexia Group	Banks – commercial and savings	Belgium
Dg Bank Group	Banks – commercial and savings	Germany
Diageo	Beverages	Britain
Dow Chemical	Chemicals	USA
Dresdner Bank	Banks – commercial and savings	Germany
Duke Energy	Energy	USA
Dynegy	Energy	USA
E.I. du Pont de Nemours	Chemicals	USA
E.ON	Trading	Germany
EADS	Aerospace and defense	Netherlands
East Japan Railway	Railroads	Japan
Eastman Kodak	Scientific, photo, control equipment	USA
Edison International	Utilities – gas and electric	USA
El Paso	Energy	USA
Electricite De France	Utilities – gas and electric	France
Electrolux	Electronics, electrical equipment	Sweden
Electronic Data Systems	Computer services and software	USA
Eli Lilly	Pharmaceuticals	USA
Emerson Electric	Electronics, electrical equipment	USA
Endesa	Utilities – gas and electric	Spain
Enel	Utilities – gas and electric	Italy

Continued

Appendix 2 Continued

Company name	Industry	Country
Eni	Petroleum refining	Italy
Enron	Energy	USA
Exxon Mobil	Petroleum refining	USA
Fannie Mae	Diversified financials	USA
Farmland Industries	Food production	USA
Faros	Diversified outsourcing services	France
Federated Department Stores	General merchandisers	USA
FedEx	Mail, package, freight delivery	USA
Fiat	Motor vehicles and parts	Italy
FleetBoston Financial	Banks – commercial and savings	USA
Fleming	Wholesalers – food and grocery	USA
Flextronics International	Electronics, electrical equipment	Singapore
Fluor	Engineering, construction	USA
Fonciere Euris	General merchandisers	France
Ford Motor	Motor vehicles and parts	USA
Fortis	Banks – commercial and savings	Belgium/ Netherlands
France Telecom	Telecommunications	France
Franz Haniel	Wholesalers – health care	Germany
Freddie Mac	Diversified financials	USA
Fuji Heavy Industries	Motor vehicles and parts	Japan
Fuji Photo Film	Scientific, photo, control equipment	Japan
Fujitsu	Computers, office equipment	Japan
Gap	Specialty retailers	USA
Gaz De France	Utilities – gas and electric	France
Gazprom	Energy	Russia
General Dynamics	Aerospace and defence	USA
General Electric	Diversified financials	USA
General Motors	Motor vehicles and parts	USA
George Weston	Food and drug stores	Canada
Georgia-Pacific	Forest and paper products	USA
GlaxoSmithKline	Pharmaceuticals	Britain
Goldman Sachs Group	Securities	USA
Goodyear Tire & Rubber	Rubber and plastic products	USA
Great Atl. & Pacific Tea	Food and drug stores	USA
Groupama	Insurance – P & C (mutual)	France
Groupe Auchan	Food and drug stores	France
Groupe Danone	Food consumer products	France
Groupe Pinault-Printemps	General merchandisers	France
Halifax	Banks – commercial and savings	Britain
Halliburton	Engineering, construction	USA

Continued

Appendix 2 Continued

Company name	Industry	Country
Hartford Financial Services	Insurance – P & C (stock)	USA
HCA	Health care	USA
Henkel	Chemicals	Germany
Hewlett-Packard	Computers, office equipment	USA
Hitachi	Electronics, electrical equipment	Japan
Home Depot	Specialty retailers	USA
Honda Motor	Motor vehicles and parts	Japan
Honeywell International	Aerospace and defence	USA
Household International	Diversified financials	USA
Hsbc Holdings	Banks – commercial and savings	Britain
Humana	Health care	USA
Hypovereinsbank	Banks – commercial and savings	Germany
Hyundai	Trading	South Korea
Hyundai Motor	Motor vehicles and parts	South Korea
IBP	Food production	USA
Idemitsu Kosan	Petroleum refining	Japan
Imperial Chemical Industries	Chemicals	Britain
Indian Oil	Petroleum refining	India
Industrial & Commercial Bank of China	Banks – commercial and savings	China
ING Group	Insurance – life, health (stock)	Netherlands
Ingram Micro	Wholesalers – electronics and office equipment	USA
Intel	Semiconductors and other electronic components	USA
International Paper	Forest and paper products	USA
Intesabci	Banks – commercial and savings	Italy
Intl. Business Machines	Computers, office equipment	USA
Invensys	Industrial and farm equipment	Britain
Isuzu Motors	Motor vehicles and parts	Japan
Itochu	Trading	Japan
Ito-Yokado	Food and drug stores	Japan
J. Sainsbury	Food and drug stores	Britain
J.C. Penney	General merchandisers	USA
J.P. Morgan Chase & Co.	Banks – commercial and savings	USA
Japan Airlines	Airlines	Japan
Japan Energy	Petroleum refining	Japan
Japan Postal Service	Mail, package, freight delivery	Japan
Japan Telecom	Telecommunications	Japan
Japan Tobacco	Tobacco	Japan
Jardine Matheson	Food and drug stores	China
Johnson & Johnson	Pharmaceuticals	USA
Johnson Controls	Motor vehicles and parts	USA

Continued

Appendix 2 Continued

Company name	Industry	Country
Jusco	Food and drug stores	Japan
Kajima	Engineering, construction	Japan
Kansai Electric Power	Utilities – gas and electric	Japan
Karstadtquelle	General merchandisers	Germany
Kawasaki Steel	Metals	Japan
Kawasho	Trading	Japan
Kddi	Telecommunications	Japan
Kimberly-Clark	Forest and paper products	USA
Kingfisher	Specialty retailers	Britain
Kinki Nippon Railway	Railroads	Japan
Kmart	General merchandisers	USA
Kobe Steel	Metals	Japan
Koninklijke Ahold	Food and drug stores	Netherlands
Korea Electric Power	Utilities – gas and electric	South Korea
Kroger	Food and drug stores	USA
Kyocera	Electronics, electrical equipment	Japan
Kyushu Electric Power	Utilities – gas and electric	Japan
L.M. Ericsson	Electronics, electrical equipment	Sweden
La Poste	Mail, package, freight delivery	France
Lafarge	Building materials, glass	France
Lagardere Groupe	Publishing, printing	France
Landesbank Baden-Wurttemberg	Banks – commercial and savings	Germany
Lear	Motor vehicles and parts	USA
Legal & General Group	Insurance – life, health (stock)	Britain
Lehman Brothers Holdings	Securities	USA
LG Electronics	Electronics, electrical equipment	South Korea
LG International	Trading	South Korea
Liberty Mutual Insurance Group	Insurance – P & C (mutual)	USA
Lloyds TSB Group	Banks – commercial and savings	Britain
Lockheed Martin	Aerospace and defense	USA
Loews	Insurance – P & C (stock)	USA
L'Oreal	Soaps, cosmetics	France
Lowe's	Specialty retailers	USA
Lucent Technologies	Network and other communications equipment	USA
Lufthansa Group	Airlines	Germany
Lukoil	Mining, crude-oil production	Russia
Magna International	Motor vehicles and parts	Canada
Man Group	Motor vehicles and parts	Germany
Manpower	Miscellaneous	USA
Marks & Spencer	General merchandisers	Britain
Marubeni	Trading	Japan
Mass. Mutual Life Insurance	Insurance – life, health (mutual)	USA

Continued

Appendix 2 Continued

Company name	Industry	Country
Matsushita Electric Industrial	Electronics, electrical equipment	Japan
Matsushita Electric Works	Electronics, electrical equipment	Japan
May Department Stores	General merchandisers	USA
Mazda Motor	Motor vehicles and parts	Japan
McDonald's	Food services	USA
McKesson HBOC	Wholesalers – health care	USA
Meiji Life Insurance	Insurance – life, health (mutual)	Japan
Merck	Pharmaceuticals	USA
Merrill Lynch	Securities	USA
MetLife	Insurance – life, health (stock)	USA
Metro	Food and drug stores	Germany
Michelin	Rubber and plastic products	France
Microsoft	Computer services and software	USA
Migros	Food and drug stores	Switzerland
Minnesota Mining & Mfg.	Scientific, photo, control equipment	USA
Mitsubishi	Trading	Japan
Mitsubishi Chemical	Chemicals	Japan
Mitsubishi Electric	Electronics, electrical equipment	Japan
Mitsubishi Heavy Industries	Industrial and farm equipment	Japan
Mitsubishi Materials	Metals	Japan
Mitsubishi Motors	Motor vehicles and parts	Japan
Mitsui	Trading	Japan
Mitsui Fudosan	Miscellaneous	Japan
Mitsui Mutual Life Insurance	Insurance – life, health (mutual)	Japan
Mizuho Holdings	Banks – commercial and savings	Japan
Montedison	Food production	Italy
Morgan Stanley Dean Witter	Securities	USA
Motorola	Network and other communications equipment	USA
Munich Re Group	Insurance – P & C (stock)	Germany
Mycal	General merchandisers	Japan
National Australia Bank	Banks – commercial and savings	Australia
Nationwide Insurance Enterprise	Insurance – P & C (stock)	USA
Nec	Electronics, electrical equipment	Japan
Nestlé	Food consumer products	Switzerland
New York Life Insurance	Insurance – life, health (mutual)	USA
News Corp.	Entertainment	Australia
Nichimen	Trading	Japan

Continued

Appendix 2 Continued

Company name	Industry	Country
Nippon Express	Mail, package, freight delivery	Japan
Nippon Life Insurance	Insurance – life, health (mutual)	Japan
Nippon Mitsubishi Oil	Petroleum refining	Japan
Nippon Steel	Metals	Japan
Nippon Telegraph & Telephone	Telecommunications	Japan
Nissan Motor	Motor vehicles and parts	Japan
Nissho Iwai	Trading	Japan
Nkk	Metals	Japan
Nokia	Electronics, electrical equipment	Finland
Nomura Securities	Securities	Japan
Norddeutsche Landesbank	Banks – commercial and savings	Germany
Norinchukin Bank	Banks – commercial and savings	Japan
Norsk Hydro	Chemicals	Norway
Nortel Networks	Network and other communications equipment	Canada
Northwest Airlines	Airlines	USA
Northwestern Mutual	Insurance – life, health (mutual)	USA
Novartis	Pharmaceuticals	Switzerland
Obayashi	Engineering, construction	Japan
Occidental Petroleum	Mining, crude-oil production	USA
Office Depot	Specialty retailers	USA
Oji Paper	Forest and paper products	Japan
Old Mutual	Insurance – life, health (stock)	South Africa
Olivetti	Telecommunications	Italy
Onex	Electronics, electrical Equipment	Canada
Otto Versand	Specialty retailers	Germany
PacifiCare Health Systems	Health care	USA
PDVSA	Petroleum refining	Venezuela
Pemex	Mining, crude-oil production	Mexico
PepsiCo	Beverages	USA
Petrobras	Petroleum refining	Brazil
Petronas	Petroleum refining	Malaysia
Peugeot	Motor vehicles and parts	France
Pfizer	Pharmaceuticals	USA
PG&E Corp.	Utilities – gas and electric	USA
Pharmacia	Pharmaceuticals	USA
Philip Morris	Tobacco	USA
Phillips Petroleum	Petroleum refining	USA
Pohang Iron & Steel	Metals	South Korea
Power Corp. of Canada	Insurance – life, health (stock)	Canada
Preussag	Miscellaneous	Germany
Procter & Gamble	Soaps, cosmetics	USA

Continued

Appendix 2 Continued

Company name	Industry	Country
Prudential	Insurance – life, health (stock)	Britain
Prudential Ins. Co. of America	Insurance – life, health (stock)	USA
Publix Super Markets	Food and drug stores	USA
Qwest Communications	Telecommunications	USA
Rabobank	Banks – commercial and savings	Netherlands
Rag	Mining, crude-oil production	Germany
Raytheon	Aerospace and defence	USA
Reliant Energy	Energy	USA
Renault	Motor vehicles and parts	France
Repsol YPF	Petroleum refining	Spain
Ricoh	Computers, office equipment	Japan
Rite Aid	Food and drug stores	USA
Robert Bosch	Motor vehicles and parts	Germany
Roche Group	Pharmaceuticals	Switzerland
Royal & Sun Alliance	Insurance – P & C (stock)	Britain
Royal Bank of Canada	Banks – commercial and savings	Canada
Royal Bank of Scotland	Banks – commercial and savings	Britain
Royal Dutch/Shell Group	Petroleum refining	Britain/ Netherlands
Royal KPN	Telecommunications	Netherlands
Royal Philips Electronics	Electronics, electrical equipment	Netherlands
RWE	Energy	Germany
Safeway	Food and drug stores	USA
Safeway	Food and drug stores	Britain
Saint-Gobain	Building materials, glass	France
Sakura Bank	Banks – commercial and savings	Japan
Samsung	Trading	South Korea
Samsung Electronics	Electronics, electrical equipment	South Korea
Samsung Life Insurance	Insurance – life, health (stock)	South Korea
Santander Central Hispano Group	Banks – commercial and savings	Spain
Sanwa Bank	Banks – commercial and savings	Japan
Sanyo Electric	Electronics, electrical equipment	Japan
Sara Lee	Food consumer products	USA
SBC Communications	Telecommunications	USA
Seagram	Entertainment	Canada
Sears Roebuck	General merchandisers	USA
Sekisui House	Engineering, construction	Japan
Sharp	Electronics, electrical equipment	Japan
Shimizu	Engineering, construction	Japan
Showa Shell Sekiyu	Petroleum refining	Japan
Siemens	Electronics, electrical equipment	Germany
Sinochem	Trading	China

Continued

Appendix 2 Continued

Company name	Industry	Country
Sinopec	Petroleum refining	China
SK	Petroleum refining	South Korea
SK Global	Trading	South Korea
Skandia Group	Insurance – life, health (stock)	Sweden
Skanska	Engineering, construction	Sweden
SNCF	Railroads	France
Snow Brand Milk Products	Food consumer products	Japan
Societe Generale	Banks – commercial and savings	France
Sodexho Alliance	Food services	France
Solectron	Semiconductors and other electronic components	USA
Sony	Electronics, electrical equipment	Japan
Southern	Utilities – gas and electric	USA
Sprint	Telecommunications	USA
Standard Life Assurance	Insurance – life, health (mutual)	Britain
Staples	Specialty retailers	USA
State Farm Insurance Cos.	Insurance – P & C (mutual)	USA
State Power	Utilities – gas and electric	China
Statoil	Petroleum refining	Norway
Stora Enso	Forest and paper products	Finland
Suez	Energy	France
Sumitomo	Trading	Japan
Sumitomo Bank	Banks – commercial and savings	Japan
Sumitomo Electric Industries	Miscellaneous	Japan
Sumitomo Life Insurance	Insurance – life, health (mutual)	Japan
Sumitomo Metal Industries	Metals	Japan
Sun Life Financial Services	Insurance – life, health (stock)	Canada
Sun Microsystems	Computers, office equipment	USA
Sunoco	Petroleum refining	USA
Suntory	Beverages	Japan
SUPERVALU	Wholesalers – food and grocery	USA
Suzuki Motor	Motor vehicles and parts	Japan
Swiss Life Ins. & Pension	Insurance – life, health (stock)	Switzerland
Swiss Reinsurance	Insurance – P & C (stock)	Switzerland
Sysco	Wholesalers – food and grocery	USA
Taisei	Engineering, construction	Japan
Taiyo Mutual Life Insurance	Insurance – life, health (mutual)	Japan
Takashimaya	General merchandisers	Japan

Continued

Appendix 2 Continued

Company name	Industry	Country
Takenaka	Engineering, construction	Japan
Target	General merchandisers	USA
Tech Data	Wholesalers – electronics and office equipment	USA
Telefonica	Telecommunications	Spain
Telstra	Telecommunications	Australia
Tenet Healthcare	Health care	USA
Tesco	Food and drug stores	Britain
Texaco	Petroleum refining	USA
Texas Instruments	Semiconductors and other electronic components	USA
Textron	Aerospace and defence	USA
Thyssen Krupp	Industrial and farm equipment	Germany
TIAA-CREF	Insurance – life, health (mutual)	USA
Tohoku Electric Power	Utilities – gas and electric	Japan
Tokio Marine & Fire Insurance	Insurance – P & C (stock)	Japan
Tokyo Electric Power	Utilities – gas and electric	Japan
Tomen	Trading	Japan
Toppan Printing	Publishing, printing	Japan
Toronto-Dominion Bank	Banks – commercial and savings	Canada
Tosco	Petroleum refining	USA
Toshiba	Electronics, electrical equipment	Japan
Total Fina Elf	Petroleum refining	France
Toyota Motor	Motor vehicles and parts	Japan
Toyota Tsusho	Trading	Japan
Toys 'R' Us	Specialty retailers	USA
Transcanada Pipelines	Energy	Canada
TRW	Motor vehicles and parts	USA
TXU	Utilities – gas and electric	USA
Tyco International	Electronics, electrical equipment	Bermuda
USA Postal Service	Mail, package, freight delivery	USA
UAL	Airlines	USA
Ubs	Banks – commercial and savings	Switzerland
Ultramar Diamond Shamrock	Petroleum refining	USA
Unicredito Italiano	Banks and commercial and savings	Italy
Unilever	Food consumer products	Britain/ Netherlands
Union Pacific	Railroads	USA
United Parcel Service	Mail, package, freight delivery	USA
United Technologies	Aerospace and defence	USA
United Health Group	Health care	USA
UNY	General merchandisers	Japan
Usinor	Metals	France
USX	Petroleum refining	USA

Continued

Appendix 2 Continued

Company name	Industry	Country
UtiliCorp United	Energy	USA
Valero Energy	Petroleum refining	USA
Verizon Communications	Telecommunications	USA
Viacom	Entertainment	USA
Vinci	Engineering, construction	France
Vivendi Universal	Engineering, construction	France
Vodafone	Telecommunications	Britain
Volkswagen	Motor vehicles and parts	Germany
Volvo	Motor vehicles and parts	Sweden
Wachovia	Banks – commercial and savings	USA
Walgreen	Food and drug stores	USA
Wal-Mart Stores	General merchandisers	USA
Walt Disney	Entertainment	USA
Washington Mutual	Banks – commercial and savings	USA
Waste Management	Miscellaneous	USA
Wells Fargo	Banks – commercial and savings	USA
West Japan Railway	Railroads	Japan
Westdeutsche Landesbank	Banks – commercial and savings	USA
Weyerhaeuser	Forest and paper products	USA
Whirlpool	Electronics, electrical equipment	USA
Williams	Energy	USA
Winn-Dixie Stores	Food and drug stores	USA
Woolworths	Food and drug stores	Australia
WorldCom	Telecommunications	USA
Xcel Energy	Utilities – gas and electric	USA
Xerox	Computers, office equipment	USA
Yasuda Fire & Marine Insurance	Insurance – P & C (stock)	Japan
Yasuda Mutual Life Insurance	Insurance – Life, Health (mutual)	Japan
Zurich Financial Services	Insurance – P & C (stock)	Switzerland

Appendix 3: Survey confidentiality statement

<u>Survey Confidentiality Statement</u>

Despite receiving full acknowledgement for having participated in the survey both you and your company can be sure that individual responses will remain wholly confidential.

The code on the reverse of your original survey is for mailing purposes only.

Initially the key containing 'name to code' linkage information will be stored separately, in a password-protected file, before being destroyed at the end of the project.

Your names, addresses and telephone numbers will be stored by me for the duration of the project and will not be passed on/sold to any other institutions or individuals.

Once you have responded I guarantee that you will not be contacted again – unless you have requested a copy of the summary report.

The returned surveys and identifying information will be shredded after the data has been entered into a database.

Once the data has been statistically analyzed it will not be possible to determine individual responses.

Arlo Brady.
May 2002.

Notes

1. Introduction

1. Despite this I cannot claim to present a completely unbiased picture – as we will discover in Chapter 3, all observations and images are tainted by what we have seen or experienced in the past (I have called this process image filtering).

2. The Rise of Corporate Conscientiousness

2. At the time of writing the cities of Seattle, Genoa and London had all experienced landmark demonstrations against among other things: globalisation, capitalism, consumerism, brands and big business – and of course the controversial US President: George W. Bush.
3. Ecological Footprinting is a methodology which measures a range of ecological impacts (e.g. waste, resource use, energy usage, etc.) and translates them into land areas. The methodology can be used to estimate the impact of (among other things) individuals, businesses, organisations and countries. The methodology assumes that society's goal is to achieve an equitable distribution of resources worldwide.
4. There are a number of publications which testify to this increase in concern, for example: DEFRA, 1998; MORI & DEFRA, 2002; Gardner, 2002; Smith, 2000. Equally one might look at the exponential increase of environmental legislation in recent years, particularly evidenced within the European Union (Haigh & Moltke, 1990).
5. A hypothetical situation whereby business is compared to the fish in a goldfish bowl – a transparent environment with no hiding places. Goldfish bowl is described by the Oxford dictionary as 'a situation lacking privacy' (Sykes, 1982).
6. For example, a report describing the second Gulf war on the US news channel ABC stated that 'The combination of satellite technology with the broad access the military is giving journalists in this war means that the reporters, photographers and camera crews 'embedded' with the troops will – in theory, at least – be able to transmit portions of the war either live, as it's happening, or within minutes or a few hours of the action taking place. ... This is going to be historic. It really is' (Kelly, 2003). It certainly was, in more ways than one; the journalist who spoke these words was tragically killed less than 24 hours later.
7. DDT was one of the most commonly used pesticides in the world prior to the early 1970s when its use was banned in most of the developed world. Despite its effectiveness as a pesticide research proved that DDT is persistent, bioaccumulative and toxic. Unfortunately, illegally and with disastrous consequences, DDT is still used in some parts of the developing world.

8. The Club of Rome is a non-profit, non-governmental organisation (NGO) and global think tank. It seeks to bring together scientists, economists, businessmen, internationally high civil servants, heads of state and former heads of state from all five continents to discuss what they call the world problematique, 'the complex set of the most crucial problems – political, social, economic, technological, environmental, psychological and cultural – facing humanity'. For further information see, www.clubofrome.org/about/ index.php
9. It is important to note that the concept of Sustainable Development has evolved from, and was primarily championed by, the environmental community. This has led to widespread misunderstanding, particularly by companies, that it refers exclusively to environmental protection. Hence the parallel, and in many cases only loosely related, development of the corporate social responsibility/citizenship movement.
10. Agenda 21 is a 'comprehensive plan of action to be taken globally, nationally and locally by organisations of the United Nations system, governments, and major groups in every area in which human impacts on the environment'. For further information see, http://www.un.org/esa/sustdev/agenda21.htm
11. See www.projectsigma.com for further details.
12. 'The natural step' is a think-tank style consultancy (now based in the US) whose raison d'etre is to encourage and facilitate global sustainability through the application of a proprietary framework. For further information see, www.naturalstep.org
13. EMAS is the European Union's voluntary Eco-Management and Audit Scheme designed to help organisations evaluate, report and improve their environmental performance, for further information see: European Commission, 2003.
14. ISO 14001 is the International Organisation for Standardisation's flagship standard for environmental management.
15. All of these companies went out of their way to support their local communities, in many cases constructing whole towns and cities to accommodate them: Cadbury's – Bournville, Lever Brothers – Port Sunlight, Toyota – Toyota City, FIAT – Turin. Lord Leverhulme (the founder of Lever Bros – the predecessor of Unilever) built Port Sunlight in Northern England as a model settlement for his employees. He guessed that workers would be more productive and loyal when offered an improved work environment and quality accommodation – and therefore he would benefit from considerable competitive advantage.
16. Except where religion was the primary driver of change – for example George Cadbury was a lifelong and dedicated Quaker.
17. Societal footprinting refers to the net positive and negative impacts of a firm on society. It is grounded in the well-developed framework of ecological footprinting, as outlined in the introduction.
18. See ILO standards on Social Security, Agriculture, Safety and Health at Work, HIV/AIDS, Child Labour, Youth Employment, Small-Scale Mining, Hotel, Catering and Tourism and Women at Work, all available online at www.ilo.org
19. For example, see the CBI's (Confederation of British Industry, see www.cbi.org.uk) stance on corporate liability for oil spills in: Friends of the Earth, 2002.

20. See the Confederation of British Industry position paper on CSR, available online at www.cbi.org.uk/csr
21. At the 2004 Detroit Motor Show the Toyota Prius was awarded the prestigious title: North American Car of the Year.
22. That is, groups of people having distinctive cultural and economic organisation (Sykes, 1982).
23. For evidence see recent MORI polls on the subject at www.mori.com
24. I have previously argued about these issues in an article that I authored for the June 2003 issue of *Clear-Profit* (www.clear-profit.com – 'From Corporate Behemoth to Friendly Hydra! How to buck the stock market by talking responsibility'.
25. Stated differently, as societies grow and become more connected with other societies – they merge to create mega-societies.
26. The minimum criteria being: 'At least two different countries must be represented in the organization and one of the representatives must not be an agent of a government' (Union of International Associations, 2002–03).
27. See the Shell/Brent Spar case in Section 3.4.
28. Esso is the trading name of the European subsidiary of Exxon Mobil Inc.
29. 'Porkies' is a Cockney rhyming slang term used in the UK to denote lies (porkies => pork pies => lies). For further information on this and other spoof adverts see, www.subvertise.org

3. Profiling Corporate Imagery: Seven Competitive Elements

30. It should be noted that for the purposes of this appraisal, organisational and corporate characteristics are jointly considered. Taken at its most basic level a company is an organisation, further analysis adds to unnecessary complication of an otherwise simple concept. I argue that as our global economy changes shape, so do companies. In an increasingly networked economy the differences between companies and organisations become progressively more difficult, and less useful to define.
31. The cynical perspective being that the campaign was designed to boost the company's visibility and reputation, while concealing its overwhelmingly dominant tobacco interests.
32. Having said this Altria are taking nothing for granted and have anticipated attacks; shortly before the name change was publicised they purchased Web domain names such as www. altriakills.com, www.altria-stinks.org and www.altriasucks.net (Smith, 2003).
33. Back in the 1980s Freeman famously defined stakeholders as 'all those who affect, or are affected by the organisation' (Freeman, 1984; Sykes, 1982). Jones took this idea further pointing out that stakeholders can be either groups or individuals (Jones, 1995).
34. 'Le client n'a jamais tort'. A quote from Cèsar Ritz, the Swiss founder of the exclusive Ritz hotels group.
35. See, http://www.dyson.com [Accessed 29th April 2002].
36. See, Gilding and Hogarth, 2000.
37. See page 26 in Shell Nigeria's 2002 'People and the Environment' annual report: Available online at: www.shell.com [Accessed 29th April 2002].

38. Year 2000 units sales from Automotive Intelligence News: Available from: www.autointell.com [Accessed 15 May 2001].
39. Year 2000 units sales from Automotive Intelligence News, excludes sales of Land Rover: Available from: www.autointell.com [Accessed May 15 2001].
40. From, http://www.reputationalquotient.com [Accessed 29 April 2002].
41. See, http://www.reputationalquotient.com [Accessed 29 April 2002].
42. See, Kevin Robert's (CEO, Saatchi & Saatchi) 'Lovemarks' theory, available from http://www.lovemarks.com [Accessed 29 April 2002].
43. For a detailed explanation of 'the triple bottom line' see Chapter 2.
44. Currently, stakeholders must rely on diverse and sometimes misleading information sources to form opinions about the intangible elements, particularly where sustainable development is concerned. Programmes like the Global Reporting Initative (GRI) aim to change this by promoting 'international harmonization in the reporting of relevant and credible corporate environmental, social and economic performance information to enhance responsible decision-making'.

4. A Global CEO Survey

45. Using an example, if, as widely predicted, global warming causes massive climatic variations, oil the primary product of today's energy-companies would represent an area of negative growth. Huge sums of money spent now in developing future reserves could be under considerable threat. Some energy companies (in the UK both Shell and BP) are clearly taking notice of this issue by investing in alternatives like solar and wind power.
46. NB: The countries of origin listed refer to those from which one or more company was asked to participate, and not necessarily those who participated.
47. The Global Business Network is 'a network of scenario professionals, connected by the open and generous exchange of ideas, "out-of-the-box" scenario thinking, ruthless curiosity, and exciting new information technologies'. More information is available on their website at www.gbn.com
48. It should be noted that my website was not online during the pre-test. A fully functioning website was launched at the beginning of February 2002 in time for the pilot test and contained a detailed explanation of the elements.
49. The surveys, both betas and the final product, and cover letters were printed on paper sourced from sustainable forests.
50. For further information see http://www.analyse-it.com/
51. See, http://www.fortune.com/fortune/global500/

5. Survey Results and Conclusions

52. Quote taken from his preface to my executive summary (see www.arlobrady.com to download the summary).
53. For a constituent country list see Section 4.2.
54. See Chapter 4 for the reasoning behind my choice of test.
55. Including the insurance sector.
56. Note that both graphs omit a scale on the X-axis, this is because of the confidentiality clause entered into with respondents. The presence of a scale would enable the identification of individual responses.

57. The term smaller is used with care, as even the smallest company in the GF500 reported 2001 revenues of US$10.3 billion.
58. I use the term 'reinforce' because the WEF survey was based on a very small sample size (36 companies) and as participants in the WEF Global Corporate Citizenship Initiative, the companies concerned were likely to be already aware of many of the challenges that sustainability issues pose.
59. The CEOs of Germany's 'Top 30' publicly traded companies (those listed in the DAX).

6. Strategic Implications

60. The 'Must' argument (the stick), the 'Should' argument (the natural inclination) and the 'Could' argument (the carrot).
61. The word sustainable is of utmost importance, because anybody can design a new PR campaign for a company – bringing obvious and immediate advantage to all concerned. However, a campaign of this nature is likely to have undesired long-term effects. Stakeholders will very quickly compare the newly presented image with the reality on the ground, picking up on any discrepancies.
62. 'Cause related branding' is a highly sophisticated branding tactic designed to increase net positive consumer perception about the responsibility of a given brand. Companies concerned support worthy causes deliberately in order to build positive brand capital. In some circles this brand association methodology is seen as a quick way to label a brand as being 'socially responsible'.
63. With the important caveat that the company should ensure that they have completed one full revolution of the virtuous responsibility circle (see Figure 2.8) before acting.
64. The UK-based Institute of Ethical and Social Accountability, headed by Dr. Simon Zadek.
65. 'Strategy 3' refers to 'Opportunity capitalisation'.
66. Corporate Citizenship.
67. Reference to the noted free-market economist of the 1970s. His concept of shareholder primacy was first outlined in a *New York Times Magazine* article on 13 September 1970: 'The Social Responsibility of Business is to Increase Its Profits'.
68. The Company Law Review – 2000.
69. It is worth noting that BT have to date relied on an independent body, AccountAbility, to facilitate their online debates – from the outset they acknowledge the fact that stakeholders do not implicitly trust them.
70. For good examples visit: www.shell.com/tellshell or www.groupbt.com/betterworld/stakeholderdialogue
71. I attribute this analogy to comments made by Joss Tantram (WWF) at a BSI meeting in London, 25th November 2003.
72. Partnerships being defined as 'some combination of public, business and civil society constituencies in voluntary, mutually beneficial, innovative relationships' (Zadek and Nelson, 2000).
73. See Chapter 2.
74. Dictionary definition, see www.m-w.com [Accessed 17 October 2003].

75. Nike, The Gap, McDonalds and others are all good examples.
76. Famous 'road maps' include those of Shell and Ford.
77. The term 'eco-efficiency' describes business activities that create economic value while reducing ecological impact and resource use (DeSimone and Popoff, 2000).
78. A reference to 'technologies such as scrubbers on smokestacks and catalytic converters on automobile tailpipes that reduce emissions of pollutants after they have formed' (European Environment Agency, 2003).
79. ISO 14001 is an international Environmental Management System standard. It provides a framework for managing environmental responsibilities so that they become more efficient and more integrated into overall business operations. [It consists of: General requirements; Environmental policy; Planning; Implementation and operation; Checking and corrective action; Management review.] For further information see www.iso.ch
80. See General Motors 2001–02 Corporate Responsibility and Sustainability Report, available online at http://gm.com/company/gmability/sustainability/reports/02/300_energy_env/320_mgmt/325_supply_chain_manage.html [Accessed 10 August 2003].
81. For example a number of companies endlessly talk about the environmental and social impact of their manufacturing processes – without showing the slightest regard for the fact that the largest environmental and social impact of their operations is during product use.
82. All of these companies went out of their way to support their local communities, in many cases constructing whole towns and cities to accommodate them: Cadbury's – Bournville, Lever Brothers – Port Sunlight, Toyota – Toyota City, FIAT – large parts of Turin.

References

AccountAbility. 2003. AA1000 series: http://www.accountability.org.uk/aa1000/default.asp

Albert, S. and Whetten, D. 1985. Organisational identity. *Research in Organisational Behaviour*, 7: 263–95.

Alsop, R. 2002. Reputations rest on good service. *The Wall Street Journal*, 16 January.

Altria Group. 2003. Corporate identity: http://www.altria.com/about_altria/01_01_corpidenchange.asp

Andriof, J. and McIntosh, M. (Eds). 2001. *Perspectives on Corporate Citizenship*. Sheffield: Greenleaf Publishing Ltd.

Armour, J., Deakin, S. and Konzelmann, S. J. 2003. Shareholder primacy and the trajectory of UK corporate governance. ESRC Centre for Business Research, University of Cambridge, Working Paper No. 266.

Arthur, W. B. 1999. Complexity and the economy. *Science*, 284: 107–9.

Ayres, R. 2003. Not to be taken for granted. *INSEAD Quarterly*, 4: 18–19.

Bachman, S. L. 2000. A new economic of child labor: searching for answers behind the headlines. *Journal of International Affairs*, 53(2): 545–77.

Baker, M. 2003. Arguments against corporate social responsibility: http://www.mallenbaker.net/csr/CSRfiles/against.html

Barker, E. 1948. *Aristotle: The Politics*. Oxford: Clarendon Press.

Barney, J. 1991. Firm resources and sustained competitive advantage. *Journal of Management*, 17: 99–120.

Barney, J. 2002. *Gaining and Sustaining Competitive Advantage*. London: Prentice Hall.

Barney, J., Wright, M. and Ketchen, D. J. 2001. The resource-based view of the firm: Ten years after 1991. *Journal of Management*, 27(6): 625–41.

Bate, R. 1995. Lessons from Brent Spar. *Economic Affairs*, 16(1): 39.

Baxter International Inc. 2001. *Sustainability Report 2001 Seeing Tomorrow Today*. Chicago: Baxter International Inc.

BBC News. 2003. SA activists hail Aids drugs U-turn: http://news.bbc.co.uk/1/hi/world/africa/3136657.stm

Bennis, W. 1997. Becoming a leader of leaders. In R. Gibson (Ed.), *Rethinking The Future*: 149–63. London: Nicholas Brealey Ltd.

Benyus, J. M. 1997. *Biomimicry: Innovation Inspired by Nature*. New York: William Morrow and Company.

Boston College. 2003. The business case for corporate citizenship: http://www.bc.edu/centers/ccc/Pages/a_aboutcc.html

Boukhari, S. 2000. Ecoprotection: an international go-slow. UNESCO Courier, May 2000.

Brady, A. 2002. Corporate reputation and sustainability; the virtuous responsibility circle. *Ethical Corporation* (October 2002): 26–28.

Brady, A. 2003. How to generate sustainable brand value from responsibility. *The Journal of Brand Management*, 10(4).

British Standards Institution. 2003 The SIGMA Guidelines – an Overview. Putting Sustainable Development into Practice – a Guide for Organisations. London.

Brookings Institute. 2000. *Understanding Intangible Sources of Value. Report of the Intangibles Task Force*. Washington, D.C.: The Brookings Institution.

Brown, B. and Perry, S. 1994. Removing the financial performance halo from Fortune's 'Most Admired' companies. *Academy of Management Journal*, 37: 1347–59.

Burston-Marsteller. 2001. *Building CEO Capital*. New York.

Bush, George. W. 2002. *The State of the Nation*. Washington: The White House.

Business Action for Sustainable Development. 2003. BASD Chief says companies have a responsibility to the communities in which they operate: http://www.basd-action.net/docs/articles/20020419_mms.shtml

Cairncross, F. 1991. *Costing the Earth; The Challenge for Governments, The Opportunities for Business*. Boston: Harvard Business School Press.

California Air Resources Board. 2003. California air quality data: http://energy.ca.gov/global_climate_change/documents/2002–07–17_AGs_LETTER.PDF

California Energy Commission. 2002. A Communication from the Chief Legal Officers of the following States: Alaska, California, Connecticut, Maine, Maryland , Massachusetts, New Hampshire, New Jersey, New York, Rhode Island, Vermont.

California Energy Commission. Assembly Bill 1493.

Carson, R. 1962. *Silent Spring*. Boston: Houghton Mifflin Company.

Castells, M. 1996. *The Rise of the Network Society*. Oxford, and Malden, MA: Blackwell Publishers.

Caves, R. 1980. Industrial organisation, corporate strategy and structure. *Journal of Economic Literature*, 18: 64–92.

Chandrasekhar, C. P. 2002. *The Economic Consequences of the Abolition of Child Labour: An Indian Case Study*. New Delhi: Centre for Economic Studies & Planning, Jawaharlal Nehru University, India.

Clifton, R. and Maughan, E. (Eds). 2000. Twenty-five visions, *The Future of Brands*. London: Interbrand and Macmillan Business.

Collins, J. and Porras, J. 1994. *Built to Last: Successful Habits of Visionary Companies*. New York: HarperCollins Inc.

Collins, J. 2000. Best beats first. Inc Magazine, August 2000: 13–14.

Collins, J. 2002. Email exchange with A. Brady (Ed.), 13 June 2002.

Cooper, D. and Schindler, P. 1998. *Business Research Methods* (sixth edn). Singapore: Irwin/McGraw-Hill.

Cooper, J. C. 1997. In the new economy, the old rules still live. *Businessweek*, 28 July.

CorpWatch.com. 2003. Greenwash: http://www.corpwatch.org/campaigns/PCC.jsp?topicid = 102

Court, D., Leiter, M. and Loch, M. 1999. Brand leverage. *The McKinsey Quarterly*, 2: 101–10.

Covey, S. 1989. *The Seven Habits of Highly Effective People*. London: Simon and Schuster Ltd.

Crosby, P. 1979a. *Quality is Free*. New York: Mc Graw Hill.

Crosby, P. 1979b. *Quality is Free; The Art of Making Quality Certain*. New York: Mc Graw Hill Inc.

Deakin, S. and Konzelmann, S. 2003. After enron: An age of enlightenment? *Organization*, 10: 583–87.

Deephouse, D. 2000. Media reputation as a strategic resource: An integration of mass communication and resource-based theories. *Journal of Management*, 26: 1091–112.

DEFRA. 1998. 1996/7. *Survey of Public Attitudes to the Environment for England and Wales*. London: Department for Environment, Food and Rural Affairs.

DEFRA. 2001. *Environmental Reporting Guidelines*. London.

DEFRA. 2002. *Survey of Public Attitudes to Quality of Life and to the Environment – 2001*. London: National Statistics Department for Environment, Food and Rural Affairs.

DeSimone, L. D. and Popoff, F. 1997. *Eco-Efficiency, The Business Link to Sustainable Development*. Cambridge MA: MIT Press.

DeSimone, L. D. and Popoff, F. 2000. *Eco-Efficiency: The Business Link to Sustainable Development*. Boston: The MIT Press.

Dillman, D. 1978. *Mail and Telephone Surveys, The Total Design Method*. New York: John Wiley and Sons.

Douglas, Alexander, A. Kanter Rosabeth Moss, Morrison Donald, Omidyar Pierre and Rifkin Jeremy. 2001. *New Economy, Old Rules?*, World Economic Forum. Davos, Switzerland.

Dowdell, T. D., Govindaraj, S. and Jain, P. C. 1992. The Tylenol incident, ensuing regulation, and stock prices. *Journal of Financial & Quantitative Analysis*, 27(2): 283–301.

Drucker, P. 1992. The new society of organisations. *Harvard Business Review*, September: 95.

Dudley, J. 2003. Theodore Roosevelt: Conservation champion and wilderness advocate. *Common Ground*, 2.1.

Eigen, P. 2001. Transparency and accountability: Preconditions for sustainability. Paper presented at the Zürich Sustainability Forum, Zürich, Switzerland.

Elkington, J. 1998. *Cannibals with Forks: The Triple Bottom Line of 21st Century Business*. Oxford, UK.: Capstone Publishing Limited.

Enderle, G. and Tavis, L. A. 1998. A balanced concept of the firm and the measurement of its long-term planning and performance. *Journal of Business Ethics*, 17: 1129–44.

Environics International. 2002. *Corporate Social Responsibility Monitor*. Toronto, Canada.

Environics Ltd. 2003. *Corporate Social Responsibility Monitor*. Toronto.

European Commission. 1999. *The Amsterdam Treaty – A Comprehensive Guide*. Brussels.

European Commission. 2003. EMAS: http://europa.eu.int/comm/environment/emas/index_en.htm

European Commission Directorate-General for Employment and Social Affairs. 2001. Pro-moting a European framework for corporate social responsibility. Green Paper. Brussels: European Commission.

European Environment Agency. 2003. EEA glossary: http://glossary.eea.eu.int/EEAGlossary/E/end-of-pipe

Eustace, C. 2000. The intangible economy impact and policy issues, report of the European high level expert group on the intangible economy. Brussels: Enterprise Directorate-General, European Commission.

Federal Reserve Board. 1999. Maintaining economic vitality: http://www.federalreserve.gov/boarddocs/speeches/1999/1990908.htm

Fill, C. and Diminopolu, E. 1999. Shaping corporate images: Attributes used to form impressions of pharmaceutical companies. *Corporate Reputation Review*, 2(3): 202–14.

Fombrun, C. and Shanley, M. 1990. What's in a name? Reputation building and corporate strategy. *Academy of Management Journal*, 33: 233–58.

Fombrun, C. 1996. *Reputation*. Boston: Harvard Business School Press.

Fortune Magazine. 2001. 2001 Fortune Global 500 database. New York.

Forum for the Future. 2003. Definitions: http://www.forumforthefuture.org.uk/whatwedo/default.asp?pageid=328

Freeman, R. E. 1984. *Strategic Management: A Stakeholder Approach*. Boston: Harper Collins.

Friedman, M. 1963. *Capitalism and Freedom*. Chicago: University of Chicago Press.

Friends of the Earth. 2002. CBI told to stop lobbying against planet: http://www.foe.co.uk/pubsinfo/infoteam/pressrel/2002/20021124223216.html

Fryxell, G. and Wang, J. 1994. The Fortune corporate 'Reputation' index: Reputation for what? *Journal of Management*, 20: 1–14.

Gardner, G. 2002. *From Rio to Johannesburg: Growing Awareness, Sluggish Response*. Washington: Worldwatch Institute, World Summit Policy Brief #1.

George, B. 2003. Why it's hard to do what's right: Today's CEOs are being swayed by every voice – except their own. *Fortune Magazine*, 15 September.

Gilding and Hogarth, 2000. We're Jammin'. Tomorrow *Magazine*, 5: 10–11.

Gioia, D. 2000. Organisational identity, image, and adaptive instability. *Academy of Management Review*, 25(1): 63–81.

Global Reporting Initiative. 2003. GRI at a glance: http://www.globalreporting.org/about/brief.asp

Golin, A. 2003. *Trust or Consequences: Build Trust Today or Lose Your Market Tomorrow*. New York: Amacom.

Gordon, L. (Ed.). 1952. *T. S. Elliot, Complete Poems and Plays: 1909–1950*. Orlando: Harcourt.

Graafland, J. J. 2002. Profits and principles: Four perspectives. *Journal of Business Ethics*, 35(4): 293–305.

Graves, S. and Waddock, S. 2000. Beyond built to last: Stakeholder relations in the built to last companies. *Business and Society Review*, 105(4): 393–418.

Greene, R. and Elffers, J. 1998. *The 48 Laws of Power*. London: Profile Books Ltd.

Grey, R. 2001. Audit your assets. *PR Week*, 7 December 2001.

Grunig, J. E. 1993. Image and Substance: From symbolic to behavioural relationships. *Public Relations Review*, 19(2): 121–39.

Habermas, J. 1964. The public sphere: An encyclopedia article. *New German Critique*, 1(3): 49–55.

Haigh and Moltke, 1990. The European Community: An environmental force. *EPA Journal* 16(4): 58–60.

Hall, R. 1992. The strategic analysis of intangible resources. *Strategic Management Journal*, 13: 135–44.

Hampden-Turner, C. and Trompenaars, F. 1997. *Mastering the Infinite Game*. London: Capstone.

Hand, J. and Lev, B. 2003. *Intangible Assets: Values, Measures and Risk*. Oxford: Oxford University Press.

Handy, C. 1997. *The Hungry Spirit*. London: Hutchinson.

Hardin, G. 1968. The tragedy of the commons. *Science*, 162: 1243–8.

Hawken, P., Lovins, A. and L. H. Lovins. 2000. *Natural Capitalism: Creating the Next Industrial Revolution*. Sheffield: Earthscan.

Held, D. 1991. Between state and civil society: Citizenship. In G. Andrews (Ed.), *Citizenship*. London: Lawrence and Wishart.

Herbig, P. and Milewicz, J. 1997. The relationship of reputation and credibility to brand success. *Journal of Pricing Strategy and Practice*, 5(1): 25–9.

HM Government. 1999. *A Strategy for Sustainable Development for the United Kingdom*. London: The Stationary Office.

Holliday, C. and Pepper, J. 2001. *Sustainability through the Market: Seven Keys to Success*. Geneva: World Business Council for Sustainable Development.

Hosmer, L. T. 1995. Trust, the connecting link between organisational theory and philosophical ethics. *Academy of Management Review*, 20(2): 379–406.

International Centre for Integrative Studies. 2000. Cloudy crystal balls: An assessment of recent European and global scenario studies and models, *Environmental Issues* Series: No 17. Copenhagen.

Jeucken, M. 2001. *Sustainable Finance and Banking*. Sheffield: Earthscan Publications Ltd.

John Foster (Ed.). 1997. *Valuing Nature? Economics, Ethics and Environment*. London: Routledge.

Johnston, P. 2001. We cannot cope without more officers, say police, *The Daily Telegraph*: 14 May. London.

Jones, T. M. 1995. Instrumental stakeholder theory. *Academy of Management Review*, 20: 404–37.

Kanter, R. M. 1996. World class leaders. In P. F. Drucker (Ed.), *The Leader of the Future*. New York: Jossey-Bass.

Kartalia, J. 2000. *Total Reputation Management*. Schaumberg, IL: Integra Corporation.

Kelly, M. 2003. *War in Real Time, ABC NEWS Report*, 19 March 2003. Northeastern Kuwait: ABC Corporation.

Kelly, Kevin. 1998. *New Rules for the New Economy: 10 Radical Strategies for a Connected World*. New York: Viking Press.

Kenyon, P. 2000. Gap and nike: No sweat?, Panorama, 15 October. London: BBC.

Kirkpatrick, D. 1990. Environmentalism: The new crusade. *Fortune Magazine* (4): 24–9.

Klein, N. 2000. *No Logo*. London: Flamingo.

Knowledge@Wharton. 2003. *Corporate Reputation: Not Worth Risking*. Pittsburgh: AON Human Capital Consulting.

KPMG and WIMM. 1999. *KPMG International Survey of Environmental Reporting*. The Hague/Amsterdam.

KPMG and UvA. 2002. *KPMG International Survey of Corporate Sustainability Reporting*. Amsterdam.

Lasn, K. 2000. *Culture Jam: How to Reverse America's Suicidal Consumer Binge – and Why We Must*. London: HarperCollins.

Laszlo, E. 2001. *Macroshift: Navigating the Transformation to a Sustainable World*. San Francisco: Berrett-Koehler Publishers, Inc.

Leadbeater, C. 2000. *Living on Thin Air: The New Economy*. London: Penguin Books.

Lissack, M., Roos, J. and Thomas, J. P. 1999. *The Next Common Sense: Mastering Corporate Complexity Through Coherence*. New York: Nicholas Brealey.

Longhurst, M. 2003. Advertising and sustainability: A new paradigm. *Admap* (July/August 2003): 44–6.

Looney, W. 1996. What the Shell Brent Spar incident means for strategists and other corporate planners. *Corporate Environmental Strategy*, 4(1): 5.

Lovelock, J. E. 1979. *Gaia: A New Look at Life on Earth*. Oxford: Oxford University Press.

Lovins, H., Lovins, A. and Weizsäcker E. von. 1998. *Factor Four: Doubling Wealth, Halving Resource Use*. Sheffield: Earthscan.

Lucier, Chuck, Eric Spiegel and Rob Schuyt. 2002. Why CEOs fall: The causes and consequences of turnover at the top. *Strategy+Business*, Third Quarter.

Lydenberg, S. D. 2003. Trust building and trust busting. *Journal of Corporate Citizenship*, 11(Autumn): 23–7.

Massie, R. K. 2001. Reporting on sustainability: A global initiative, *OECD Reporter*, Vol. 15, June 2001.

McIntosh, M., Leipziger, D., Jones, K. and Coleman, G. 1998. Corporate Citizenship. Successful strategies for responsible companies. *Financial Times*: London.

McLane, P., Bratic, W. and Bersin, B. 1999. Potentially devastating events. How three companies managed and survived a crisis. *Corporate Reputation Review*, 2(3): 268–77.

Meadows, D. L. 1972. *The Limits to Growth*. New York: Universe Books.

Mokyr, J. 2002. *The Gifts of Athena: Historical Origins of the Knowledge Economy*. Princeton: Princeton University Press.

Morsing, M. 2003. Conspicuous responsibility. In C. Thyssen (Ed.), *Corporate Values and Responsibility*. Fredriksberg: Samfundslitteratur.

Muller, H. 2001. Winds of change. *Fortune*, 143(6): 30–40.

Muller-Kraenner, S. 2002. On the road to Johannesburg. *Development*, 45(3): 18–23.

Munro, D. A. and Martin W. Holdgate (Eds). 1991. *Caring for the Earth: A Strategy for Sustainable Living*. Gland, Switzerland: The World Conservation Union/United Nations Environment Programme/World Wide Fund for Nature.

Murphy, C. 2002. Is BP beyond petroleum? Hardly. *Fortune Magazine*, 146(6).

Nanus, B. 1995. *Visionary Leadership*. San Francisco: Jossey-Bass.

Nolan, J. 1975. Protect your public image with performance. *Harvard Business Review* (March–April).

OECD. 2000. Is there a new economy? First report on the OECD growth project. Paris.

Oliviero, M. and Simmons, A. 2002. Who's minding the store? Global civil society and corporate responsibility. In H. Anheier (Ed.), *Global Civil Society* 2002: 77–107. Oxford: Oxford University Press.

Palast, G. 2002. *The Best Democracy Money Can Buy*. London: Pluto Press.

Pearce, David, Anil Markandya, and Barbier, E. B. (Eds). 1989. *Blueprint for a Green Economy*. Sheffield: Earthscan.

Peters, G. 1999. *Waltzing With the Raptors: A Practical Roadmap To Protecting your Company's Reputation*. New York: John Wiley & Sons Inc.

Petrick, J., Scherer, R., Brodzinski, J., Quinn, J. and Ainina, M. 1999. Global leadership skills and reputational capital: Intangible resources for sustainable competitive advantage. *The Academy of Management Executive*, 13(1): 58–69.

Plender, J. 1997. *A Stake in the Future*. London: Nicholas Brealey Publishing Ltd.

Porter, M. and Kramer, M. 2002. The competitive advantage of corporate philanthropy. *Harvard Business Review*, 80(12): 57–68.

Post, J. E. 2002. Global corporate citizenship: Principles to live and work by. *Business Ethics Quarterly*, 12(2): 143–53.

Pratkanis, A. and Aronson, E. 1991. *Age of Propaganda. The Everyday Use and Abuse of Persuasion*. New York: W H Freeman and Company.

PricewaterhouseCoopers. 2003a. *Management Barometer*. New York.

PricewaterhouseCoopers. 2003b. Sixth annual global CEO survey. Leadership, responsibility and growth in uncertain times.

PRWeek/Burson Marsteller. 2002. CEOs building credibility from the inside out., *PRWeek*, Vol. 11, November 2002.

Rigdon, J. I. 2000. The second-mover advantage; Why it pays to let pioneers make the mistakes. *Red Herring Magazine*, September.

Robèrt, K.-H. 2002. *The Natural Step Story: Seeding a Quiet Revolution*. British Colombia, Canada: New Society Publishers.

Robèrt, K.-H., Schmidt-Bleek, B., Larderel, J. A. d., Basile, G., Jansen, J. L., Kuehr, R., Thomas, P. P., Suzuki, M., Hawken, P. and Wackernagel, M. 2002. Strategic sustainable development – selection, design and synergies of applied tools. *Journal of Cleaner Production*, 10(3): 197–214.

Roberts, S., Keeble, J. and Brown, D. 2002. *The Business Case for Corporate Citizenship*. Cambridge: Arthur D Little.

Roddick, A. 1992. *Body and Soul*. London: Vermilion.

Ryan, C. 2002. *Sustainable Consumption: A Global Status Report*. Paris: United Nations Environment Programme: Division of Technology, Industry and Economics, Production and Consumption Branch.

Schoemaker, P. 1995. Scenario planning: A tool for strategic thinking. *Sloan Management Review*, 36(2).

Schwartz, P. 1991. *The Art of the Long View*. London: Century Business.

Scott, S. and Lane, V. 2000. A stakeholder approach to organisational identity. *Academy of Management Journal*, 25(1): 43–62.

Sd3 Ltd. 2003. What is sustainability? http://www.sd3.co.uk/sustainability.html

Sehested, K. 2003. Cross-sector partnerships as a new form of local governance. In L. Kjaer (Ed.), *Local Partnerships in Europe*. Copenhagen: The Copenhagen Centre.

Shell International. 1998. *The Shell Report 1998: Profits and Principles, Does There Have To Be a Choice?* London: Shell International.

Shell International. 1999. *The Shell Report 1999: People, Planet & Profits; an Act of Commitment*. London: Shell International.

Smith, C. 1994. The new corporate philanthropy. *Harvard Business Review*, 72(3): 105–16.

Smith, E. A. and Malone, R. E. 2003. Altria means tobacco: Philip Morris's identity crisis. *American Journal of Public Health*, 93(4).

Smith, J. (Ed.). 2000. *The Daily Globe: Environmental Change, the Public and the Media*. London: Earthscan Ltd.

Social Investment Forum. 2001. *2001 Report on Socially Responsible Investing Trends in the United States*. Washington, DC.

Soros, G. 2002. *George Soros on Globalisation*. London: Public Affairs.

Sparkes, R. 2002. *Socially Responsible Investment: A Global Revolution*. London: Wiley.

Sternberg, E. 1998. *Stakeholding: Betraying the Corporation's Objectives*. London: The Social Affairs Unit.

Stewart, T. A. 2001. *The Wealth of Knowledge: Intellectual Capital and the Twenty-first Century Organization*. New York: Doubleday & Company.

Stiglitz, J. 2003. *Globalisation and its Discontents*. London: Penguin.

SustainAbility Ltd, UNEP, IISD and Deloitte Touche. 1993. *Coming Clean*. London.

SustainAbility Ltd and UNEP. 1996. *Engaging Stakeholders (Volumes 1 & 2)*. London.

SustainAbility Ltd and UNEP. 1997. *The 1997 Benchmark Survey*. London.

SustainAbility Ltd and UNEP. 1998. *The Non-Reporters Report*. London.

SustainAbility Ltd and UNEP. 2000. *The Global Reporters*. London.

SustainAbility Ltd. 2003. What is the triple bottom line? http://www.sustainability.com/philosophy/triple-bottom/tbl-intro.asp

Sykes, J. B. (Ed.). 1982. *The Concise Oxford Dictionary of Current English*. Oxford: Oxford University Press.

The Centre for Business Performance. 2001. *Briefing 08.01: Sustainability and Corporate Reputation*. London: The Institute of Chartered Accountants in England and Wales.

The Club of Rome. 2003. About us: http://www.clubofrome.org/about/index.php

The Conference Board. 2002. The CEO challenge: *Top Marketplace and Management Issues-2002*. New York.

The Economist. 2001. Helping, but not developing, *The Economist*: 12 May.

The Economist. 2002. The unlikeliest scourge. *The Economist*, 13 July.

The Economist. 2003. The unrepentant oilman. *The Economist*, 15 March.

The Institute of Chartered Accountants. 1999. *Internal Control: Guidance for Directors on the Combined Code*. London.

TNS Emnid. 2001. *Germany's Top Managers – Charisma is Capital*. Wirtschaftswoche.

Tonn, B. E. 1999. sustainability and supra-communitarianism. *Foresight*, 1(4): 343–52.

Turban, D. B. and Greening, D. W. 1997. Corporate social performance and organizational attractiveness to prospective employees. *The Academy of Management Executive*, 13(1): 58–69.

UK Social Investment Forum. 2003. SRI markets: http://www.uksif.org/Z/Z/Z/sri/mkts/index.shtml#meth

Union of International Associations. 2002–03. Yearbook of international organisations: http://www.uia.org/organizations/

United Nations Conference on Trade and Development. 2001. *World Investment Report 2001: Promoting Linkages*. New York and Geneva: UNCTAD.

United Nations Development Programme, United Nations Environment Programme, World Bank and World Resources Institute. 2003a. Awakening civil society. In WRI (Ed.), *World Resources 2002–2003*: 65–88. Washington: World Resources Institute.

United Nations Environment Programme. 1997. *UNEP Statement by Financial Institutions on the Environment & Sustainable Development*. Geneva.

Van Ham, P. 2001. The rise of the brand state. *Foreign Affairs* (September–October).

Viederman, S. 1996. Sustainability's five capitals and three pillars. In D. Pirages (Ed.), *Building Sustainable Societies: A Blueprint for a Post-Industrial World*. Armonk, New York: ME Sharpe.

Wackernagel, M., Schulz, N. B., Deumling, D., Linares, A. C., Jenkins, M., Kapos, V., Monfreda, C., Loh, J., Myers, N., Norgaard, R. and Randers, J. 2002. Tracking the ecological overshoot of the human economy. *Proceedings of the National Academy of Sciences*, 99(14): 9266–71.

Waddock, S. 2001. *Leading Corporate Citizens*. Columbus, OH: Irwin/McGraw Hill.
Waddock, S., Bodwell, C. and Graves, S. 2002. Responsibility: the new business imperitive. *Academy of Management Executive,* 16(2): 132–48.
Wartick, L. 2002. Measuring corporate reputation, definition and data. *Business and Society,* 41(4): 371–92.
Watts, P. and Holme, R. 1999. *CSR: Meeting Changing Expectations*. Geneva: World Business Council for Sustainable Development.
Watts, P. and Holme, R. 2000. *CSR: Making Good Business Sense*. Geneva: World Business Council for Sustainable Development.
WCED. 1987. *Our Common Future*. Oxford University Press.
Weber, M. 1947. *The Theory of Social and Economic Organization*. New York: The Free Press.
Werner-felt, B. 1984. A resource-based view of the firm. *Strategic Management Journal,* 5: 171–80.
Willmott, M. 2001. *Citizen Brands: Putting Society at the Heart of Business*. Chichester, UK: John Wiley & Sons.
Willums, J. -O. 1998. *The Sustainable Business Challenge, A Briefing for Tomorrow's Business Leaders*. Sheffield, UK.
Wilson, E. 1998. The biological basis of morality. *The Atlantic Monthly*(April).
Wolf, M. 2002. Countries Still Rule the World. *Financial Times,* 6 February 2002.
Womack, J. P. and Jones, D. T. 1996. *Lean Thinking*. New York: Simon & Schuster.
World Bank. 2003. Environmental valuation: http://Inweb18.worldbank.org/ESSD/essdext.nsf/44ByDocName/EnvironmentalEconomicsandItsApplications EnvironmentalValuation
World Business Council for Sustainable Development. 2003. FAQs about the WBCSD: http://www.wbcsd.org/templates/TemplateWBCSD1/layout.asp?type = p&MenuId = Mjk0&doOpen = 1&ClickMenu = LeftMenu#2
World Commission on Environment Development (WCED). 1987. *Our Common Future*. Oxford and New York: Oxford University Press. p. 400.
World Economic Forum. 2002. *CEO Survey on Global Corporate Citizenship*. Geneva.
World Summit on Sustainable Development. 2002. *FACTS ABOUT: Poverty and the Millennium Development Goals*. Johannesburg: World Summit on Sustainable Development.
Zadek, S. 2001. *The Civil Corporation*. London: Earthscan Publications.
Zadek, S. and Nelson, J. 2000. *Partnership Alchemy*. Copenhagen: The Copenhagen Centre.

Index